£2-20

D0571485

THE COMMONWEALTH AND INTERNATIONAL LIBRARY

Joint Chairmen of the Honorary Editorial Advisory Board

SIR ROBERT ROBINSON, O.M., F.R.S., LONDON
DEAN ATHELSTAN SPILHAUS, MINNESOTA

Publisher: ROBERT MAXWELL, M.C., M.P.

BOTANY DIVISON

General Editors: G. F. ASPREY, J. BRADY and A. G. LYON

FLORAL BIOLOGY

MARY PERCIVAL

FLORAL
BIOLOGY

THE QUEEN'S AWARD
TO INDUSTRY 1966

PERGAMON PRESS

OXFORD · LONDON · EDINBURGH · NEW YORK
TORONTO · SYDNEY · PARIS · BRAUNSCHWIEG

MIDDLEBURY COLLEGE LIBRARY

Pergamon Press Ltd., Headington Hill Hall, Oxford
4 & 5 Fitzroy Square, London W.1
Pergamon Press (Scotland) Ltd., 2 & 3 Teviot Place, Edinburgh 1
Pergamon Press Inc., Maxwell House, Fairview Park, Elmsford,
New York 10523
Pergamon of Canada Ltd., 207 Queen's Quay West, Toronto 1
Pergamon Press (Aust.) Pty. Ltd., 19a Boundary Street,
Rushcutters Bay, Sydney, N.S.W. 2011, Australia
Pergamon Press S.A.R.L., 24 rue des Écoles, Paris 5ᵉ
Vieweg & Sohn GmbH, Burgplatz 1, Braunschweig

Copyright © 1965 Pergamon Press Ltd.

*All Rights Reserved. No part of this publication may be reproduced,
stored in a retrieval system, or transmitted, in any form or by any
means, electronic, mechanical, photocopying, recording, or otherwise,
without the prior permission of Pergamon Press Limited.*

First edition 1965

Reprinted with corrections 1969

Library of Congress Catalog Card No. 64-18202

Printed in Great Britain by A. Wheaton & Co., Exeter

This book is sold subject to the condition
that it shall not, by way of trade, be lent,
resold, hired out, or otherwise disposed
of without the publisher's consent,
in any form of binding or cover
other than that in which
it is published.

08 010609 9   (flexicover)
08 010610 2   (hard cover)
08 010611 0   (flexicover non-net)

Dedication

To Professor Emeritus R. C. McLean

CONTENTS

ACKNOWLEDGMENTS

THE AUTHOR would like to tender her grateful thanks to Miss Patricia Morgan, who collected the data of Tables 1, 3 and 7 and also helped with the illustrations and literature: to Dr. A. G. Lyon, who took the photographs: to Miss G. M. Granger, who drew *Leonotis leonurus*: and to Mr. C. McCann, for permission to reproduce his drawing of the Tui. Their contributions speak for themselves and their kindness and willingness to help has been greatly appreciated.

She would also like to thank Dr. W. C. Osman Hill who provided the birds for examination, and Dr. E. G. Linsley who gave the specimens of *Onagrandrena*.

INTRODUCTION

DEFINITION OF FLORAL BIOLOGY

Floral Biology is the science of flower life, a life that begins with the ripening of one or other of the essential organs, such as the dehiscence of the first stamen or the attainment of receptivity by a stigma, and ends when the stamens have shed all their pollen and the stigmas cease to be receptive. All events before this, the opening of the calyx and corolla, the extension and orientation of their members, occur, strictly speaking, before the real life begins, and fertilization and the changes accompanying it, are, in their turn, post-floral. In this book, the latter will be omitted, but, as the former events often have an important bearing on the life of the flower, they will be included.

THE HISTORY OF FLORAL BIOLOGY AND SCOPE OF THE BOOK

The history of Floral Biology dates from the researches and observations of Christian Conrad Sprengel contained in his book *The Secret of Nature in the Form and Fertilization of Flowers Discovered*, published in 1793. His observations of flowers led him to realize that certain features, such as the protection of the nectaries by hairs, the presence of nectar guides on petals, and the bright colours of the petals themselves were there for the purpose of attracting insects to the flowers to pollinate them. It is remarkable that he did not also perceive that cross-pollination is an advantage to the plants, for, in the introduction to his book he says "Since very many flowers are of one sex only, and probably many more are dichogamous, nature seems to intend that no flower shall be fertilized by means of its own pollen". He had even shown by experiment that *Hemerocallis fulva*, the Day Lily is self-sterile. This failure led to the neglect of his work for 70 years, and its true value was not realized until after the publication of Darwin's *Origin of Species*, when the theory of natural selection brought it into prominence. Then came Darwin's classic studies *The Various Contrivances by which Orchids are Fertilized by Insects*, 1862, and *The Different Forms of Flowers on Plants of the Same Species*, 1880.

In 1873 Herman Müller published *The Fertilization of Flowers*. The English translation by D'Arcy Thompson appeared 10 years later and contained all the author's additional references up to that date. This was followed by Kerner's *The Natural History of Plants*, 1894–5 and P. Knuth's *Handbook of Flower Pollination*, 1898. These books are the great treasure houses of floral biological data. Nowhere else is there such a wealth of factual knowledge. This has recently been supplemented by Dr. Hans Kugler's *Einführung in die Blütenekologie* (1955) and Dr. Stefan Vogel's review *Blütenbiologische Typen als Elemente der Sippengliederung* (1954).

The present book is an attempt to present the subject in such a way that it may attract new workers, who, armed with the new techniques, and stimulated by the findings of recent investigators may be able to carry the science of Floral Biology forward into new fields.

With this aim in view, an attempt has been made, wherever it has been possible, to show how the modern floral biologists have conducted their experiments and state what techniques they have employed. The great simplicity and ingenuity of these methods are in themselves a delight. This *is* a field where simple observations, undertaken in an intelligent manner by anyone, schoolchild, science student and layman alike, may yield valuable data, and, moreover, will prove immensely satisfying to the investigator. Embracing, as it does, both the animal and plant kingdoms, it is perhaps the ideal biological subject for schools. The techniques employed include those of physics, chemistry, physiology and psychology, genetics and ecology, and so constitute a broad training in biology, which may be useful and acceptable in other fields. Conversely, anyone with specialist knowledge will be able, should he so choose, to make a contribution to the subject.

Some hints for students as to the tools required, how to make them, and a schedule of procedure for the study of the floral biology of a species, are given in the last chapter.

References, as well as a bibliography, have been listed, firstly, so that students may know exactly where to find a paper that interests them, and secondly, that they may be encouraged to read the original papers. Nowadays, most papers in other languages have English summaries, so that there need be no hesitation in consulting these too.

CHAPTER I

SEX IN FLOWERS

A FLOWER is defined as "a collection of essential organs, of stamens or pistils or both, with protective envelopes". It is a specialized structure, in which the same tissue cannot produce both male and female organs and therefore a **space barrier** exists between them. It is because of this that pollination is necessary. The gap may be greater or less depending upon the distribution of sex in the species.

SEX DISTRIBUTION IN PLANTS

The sex of flowers is determined *genetically* but environmental factors govern its *expression*. These are sometimes nutritional, sometimes a function of the photoperiod (i.e. the length of daylight a plant receives each day), and sometimes dependent on the intensity of light which the plant is receiving. Some workers are investigating the experimental control of sex expression in economic crops.

Arisaema triphyllum (Araceae) is usually dioecious, but if the plants are cut back severely and grown under droughty conditions, the next season's flowers will all be male. If they are well watered and manured the next crop of flowers will be female. *Carica papaya*, the PawPaw, reacts similarly.

Cucurbitas, supplied with abundant nitrogen and grown under conditions of short photoperiod and low night temperatures (10°C), produce more female flowers than male, whereas "long day" treatment resulted in more male flowers (Heslop-Harrison, 1957).

1

In some succulents a low light intensity during the flowering period suppressed the development of stamens (Resende, 1950).

The majority of angiosperm flowers are hermaphrodite. The suppression of either sex, resulting in the production of a unisexual flower, is considered to be a derived state. Often the suppression is incomplete, staminodes are present in the female flower and infertile or rudimentary ovaries in the male, which gives weight to this view.

FIG. 1. *Plantago lanceolata* hermaphrodite inflorescence in anthesis. The anthers are versatile and the pollen dry coated. Honey-bees collect large loads after wetting it with regurgitated honey. ×1·6.

TERMINOLOGY

Plants with hermaphrodite flowers are termed **monoclinous**. Plants with male and female flowers are termed **diclinous**.

A diclinous plant with male and female flowers on the same plant is **monoecious**.

A diclinous plant with male and female flowers on different plants is **dioecious**.

A species in which all the plants bear both hermaphrodite and female flowers is **gynomonoecious**; those with all plants bearing hermaphrodite and male flowers, **andromonoecious**, and those with all plants bearing hermaphrodite, male and female flowers, **trimonoecious**.

If a species has some plants with only hermaphrodite flowers and others with only female flowers, it is **gynodioecious**; if it has hermaphrodite and male flowered plants, it is **androdioecious**, and if it has separate hermaphrodite, male and female flowered plants, it is **trioecious**.

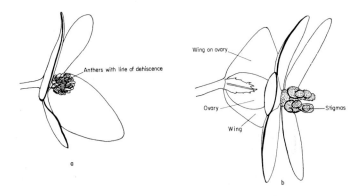

Fig. 2. *Begonia*, a monoecious species. a. Male flower in anthesis. b. Female flower with inferior winged ovary and yellow velvety stigmas which resemble superficially the cone of stamens. Both flowers are nectarless. ×3.

These distinctions are not absolute. The Ribwort Plantain, *Plantago lanceolata* (Fig. 1) shows several intergradations from fully hermaphrodite to purely female flowers in different individuals. The Bladder Campion, *Silene vulgaris* has five kinds of plant; male, andromonoecious, female, gynomonoecious and hermaphrodite.

Monoclinous plants include species of *Magnolia, Ranunculus, Papaver, Rosa, Pyrus, Prunus, Brassica, Lilium* and *Passiflora*. **Monoecious** plants include a large group of species of wind pollinated genera such as *Corylus, Alnus, Betula, Quercus* and *Fagus*. The Cucurbitaceae (Vegetable Marrow, Melon, Cucumber) and the Begoniaceae (Fig. 2), are also monoecious. A well-

3

Fig. 3a. *Aesculus hippocastanum*, andromonoecious species. Male flowers: lowest, youngest flower has yellow nectar guide at base of the two upper petals (no contrast for film). Left hand flower; nectar guides orange, and top right, oldest flower, guides deep pink. The orange and pink guides have different scents. ×1·7.

known **dioecious** group is that of the willows (*Salix*) and poplars (*Populus*). The Red Campion (*Silene dioica*), the Stinging Nettle (*Urtica dioica*), and the Holly (*Ilex aquifolium*) are strictly dioecious. *Syringa persica* and *Parietaria diffusa* (Pellitory-of-the-Wall), are **gynomonoecious**, and the latter shows a secondary sex character, in that the perianth of the

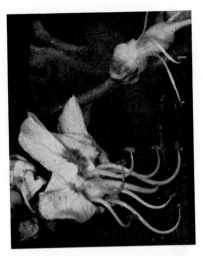

Fig. 3b. *Aesculus hippocastanum*, andromonoecious species. Hermaphrodite flower, late stage; anther dehiscence complete and nectar guide deep pink. At this stage the sepals reflex enabling *Bombus terrestris* to exploit flower from the back. Above right, an old flower with swelling ovary and completely reflexed sepals. × 1·7.

female flower is tubular, with four teeth, while the hermaphrodite flowers have four separate sepals. Male flowers may also occur, in which case the plant becomes **trimonoecious**. *Poterium sanguisorba* (Salad Burnet), another trimonoecious species, has flowers massed in rounded heads. The lowermost are male, the middle hermaphrodite and the topmost female. *Aesculus hippocastanum*, the Horse Chestnut, is **andromonoecious**; there are more male than hermaphrodite flowers on the candle-like inflorescence and the former begin to flower first (Fig. 3a and b).

Glechoma hederacea, the Ground Ivy, is **gynodioecious**. The female plant is a little less robust than the hermaphrodite and

Fig. 4. *Glechoma hederacea*, gynodioecious species. Female flower, lower lip 3·7 mm in width, corolla tube 4 mm. Two curved stigmas held well before mouth of corolla.

Fig. 5. *Glechoma hederacea*, hermaphrodite flowers which are larger (lower lip 6·7 mm wide) and longer (corolla tube 8·5 mm) than the female flower. Typical nototribic bee flower with landing platform, hidden nectar and central tongue-guide between hair fringes on lower lip.

comes into flower somewhat earlier. The flowers are very different in size. The females are narrower across the petals and have shorter tubes, 3·7 mm and 4 mm respectively (Fig. 4), as against 6·7 mm and 8·5 mm for the hermaphrodites (Fig. 5). This may very well set up a mechanical barrier to pollination between the two plants. A pollinator of medium tongue-length, such as the honey-bee, would scarcely be able to reach the nectar in the bisexual flower, and might well confine her visits to the female plant alone, thus rendering ineffective the mechanism for outbreeding which this type of sex distribution should ensure. Gynodioecism in this species appears to be due to a virus-like particle in the cytoplasm of the female plant, for if the female is grafted on to the hermaphrodite plant, the latter becomes female.

Caltha palustris (Marsh Marigold) is sometimes **andro-dioecious**, and sometimes andromonoecious. *Empetrum nigrum* has been considered **trioecious**, that is having three differently sexed plants, male, female and hermaphrodite. This is probably incorrect and arises from the confusion between *E. nigrum* which is dioecious and *E. hermaphroditum* which has bisexual flowers.

TYPES OF POLLINATION

AUTOGAMY AND ALLOGAMY

If a flower receives its own pollen it is **self-pollinated**, and if this leads to successful fertilization, it is termed **autogamy**. If a flower receives pollen from another flower, it is **cross-pollinated**. Successful fertilization, following cross-pollination, is termed **allogamy**; between two flowers on the *same* plant it is **Geito-nogamy**; between two flowers on *separate* plants, **Xenogamy**, and between two flowers of *separate species*, **hybridization**.

Provision for cross-pollination may be made within the individual flower in one of two ways, either the stamens and stigmas are widely separated in space (Fig. 6), or they ripen at different times. Both features may be present in one flower.

HOMOGAMY

When stigmas and anthers mature simultaneously the flower is said to be **homogamous**. Potentially these flowers can be self-fertilized.

7

DICHOGAMY

When stigmas and anthers mature at different times, the flowers are called **dichogamous**. Flowers with the anthers ripening first are **protandrous**, those with the stigmas becoming receptive first, **protogynous**. Protandry is a marked feature of the Compositae, Campanulaceae and Umbelliferae, also of the genera *Geranium*, *Pelargonium* and *Malva*. *Helleborus*, *Magnolia*,

FIG. 6. Apple, dichogamous flower; anther dehiscence already completed and styles well above anthers with stigmas in the receptive state.
× 2.

Aristolochia and *Scrophularia* are protogynous. Varieties of pear differ in the order of ripening and in the relative height of stamens and stigmas. Srivastava (1937) observed that Conference, Comice and Pitmaston Duchess are all protandrous. In Conference the styles are longer than the stamens, in Comice they are shorter, in Pitmaston Duchess the styles equal the stamens. Beurre Hardy is homogamous, but the styles are longer than the stamens. As Comice and Pitmaston Duchess are self-sterile, their dichogamy is a needless precaution against self-fertilization. Beurre Hardy, too, is self-sterile and therefore not functionally homogamous. Conference is self-fertile and the stigmas ripen before anther dehiscence is complete, enhancing the possibility of self-pollination.

CHASMOGAMY AND CLEISTOGAMY

Flowers may be primarily divided into those which open and expose their stamens and stigmas to the air, i.e. chasmogamic, and those which remain closed and are necessarily self-fertilized. The majority of angiosperms are chasmogamic and as their structure and attributes form the main part of the text, they will not be considered further here.

Cleistogamy is the descriptive term for the phenomenon of seed-set without the flowers coming into bloom. Cleistogamous flowers fail to open, yet produce good seed. An obvious condition of cleistogamy is autogamy, for no plant which is self-sterile can reap any benefit from it. In Hungary, some individuals of *Robinia pseudacacia* are persistently cleistogamous. As the species is self-sterile, they set no seed. Cleistogamy is a widespread natural phenomenon, occurring in such mesophytic plants as our native *Viola odorata*, *Oxalis acetosella* and the grass *Sieglingia decumbens*; but more often it is brought about by severe environmental conditions, in which case it is termed **ecological** cleistogamy (Uphof, 1938).

FEATURES OF CLEISTOGAMOUS FLOWERS

Cleistogamous flowers may only differ from the normal ones of the species in that the petals remain closed. Such are those of *Purpurella cleistoflora* (Melastomaceae) in Brazil. These, however, have a very curious floral biology, for they are visited by robber bumble-bees which force an entrance (to exploit the pollen), and in doing so pollinate the stigmas. This is a rare case in that the potentiality for cross-pollination is not lost.

FLORAL MODIFICATIONS ASSOCIATED WITH CLEISTOGAMY

Many cleistogamous flowers are modified to a greater or lesser degree and often have the appearance of buds whose development has been arrested. The calyx seldom changes, nor does the ovary, but the intermediate whorls usually suffer reduction. Those of *Specularia perfoliata* are exceptional in having fewer carpels than the chasmogamic flowers. In *Cardamine chenopodifolia*,

9

whose cleistogamic flowers are subterranean, the petals are tiny and colourless and may be missing altogether; and in *Viola odorata* too the petals are small. Petals of cleistogamic flowers usually lose their scent, but this is not the case in the violet for the whole plant appears to be scented. Nectaries, too, disappear from the flower, but again we have an exception in *Myrmecodia tuberosa* (Rubiaceae) (Burck, 1890), where the nectar, which cannot be exploited because of the flower's cleistogamy, rises to a third of the length of the corolla tube.

The cleistogamic flowers of *Oxalis acetosella* have fewer stamens than the normal ones. The anther wall may also be modified as in *Amphicarpaea monoica* (Papilionaceae), where it lacks the fibrous layer which is a part of the opening mechanism in normal flowers. There is also a tendency for a reduction in the number of pollen grains, for example from thousands per flower to a mere two hundred in *Viola canina*. The biology of the androecium and pollen of *V. odorata* var. *praecox* has been elucidated by Madge (1929). The plant produces three kinds of flowers, chasmogamic, semicleistogamic and cleistogamic. All of them have two kinds of pollen grains in the anthers: these differ both morphologically and biologically. They are (a) ovoid or tetrahedral and (b) round ridged. The latter may be immature ovoid grains. Much of the pollen germinates *within* the anthers in all three types of flowers, but in the cleistogamic and semicleistogamic the round ridged grains germinate and their pollen tubes grow through the anther walls to the stigmas. In the chasmogamic it is the ovoid grains which germinate, but the tubes mostly stay within the anther. *V. riviniana* also has dimorphic pollen, of large and small grains. In the chasmogamic flowers the former become free, and are available for transference by insects, while the latter germinate inside the anthers. The cleistogamic produce the small-sized grains.

Some flowers are **facultative** cleistogams. Those of *Sieglingia decumbens*, a common grass in coastal areas, usually remain closed, yet in Wales they occasionally open and render cross-pollination possible. This plant also has a tiny, colourless, cleistogamic flower tucked away at the bottom of the sheath of the lowest leaf of the stem.

Most terrestrial orchids are geophytes, that is they perennate the greater part of the year by means of underground tubers; but the whole of the life history, *including the flowering*, is carried out below ground in the two remarkable Australian orchids, *Cryptanthemis slateri* and *Rhizanthella gardneri*. It is not specifically stated whether the flowers themselves are cleistogamous.

ECOLOGICAL CLEISTOGAMY

Almost any factor of the environment may prevent normal chasmogamic flowering in a particular species: areas where such conditions persist for long periods are inhabited by a greater proportion of plants which have the faculty of producing cleistogamous flowers.

ENVIRONMENTAL FACTORS INDUCING CLEISTOGAMY

Lack of water, or water in excess may both induce cleistogamy. *Ranunculus moseleyi*, during periods of flooding, produces aerial chasmogamic flowers with yellow petals which bear the usual nectar pocket at the base, and greenish cleistogamic ones below water which are nectarless. Excessive atmospheric moisture also causes cleistogamy. When growing in the wet and misty rain forest, the orchid, *Liparis caespitosa*, is cleistogamous, but if it is growing in the drier air outside the trees it is chasmogamic.

Drought, combined with heat, may prevent chasmogamy and normal plant–insect relations. Such is the case at Timbuctu (Hagerup, 1932) where the ground temperatures are in the region of 70–80°C throughout the year. Pollinating insects cannot live in such heat, and the ground flora consists of species which have become cleistogamous and self-pollinating which is the only mode of flower life possible for them. This is all the more remarkable as many of them belong to families which are typically entomophilous, such as the Leguminosae and Polygalaceae (*Polygala triflora*), which both have the familiar zygomorphic papilionate facies, and Onagraceae (*Jussiaea acuminata*) which is also especially associated with the solitary bees. *Commelina forskålei* Vahl, a member of the Commelinaceae, a family we usually associate with the moist sub-tropical rain forests as a ground carpeter, here reproduces successfully in this condition of extreme heat by means of a cleistogamous

11

flower which is completely enclosed in an enveloping involucre filled with slime. These involucres are borne on slender runners below ground level, and resemble at first sight, turions (the winter buds of aquatic plants). The plant also produces pairs of flowers, similarly protected by a folded slime-filled leaf, above ground. These are hermaphrodite, one is chasmogamic, the other cleistogamic. Despite this, *both* are self-pollinated and self-fertile.

SEASONAL CLEISTOGAMY

Viola odorata exhibits seasonal cleistogamy. The main crop of chasmogamic flowers is produced in the spring, and these are succeeded in summer by the cleistogamic ones which remain hidden among the foliage and set abundant good seed. A curious state of affairs exists in *Aechmanthera wallichii* var. *gossypina* (Acanthaceae). During the cold season in India it has large chasmogamic flowers, but these are **sterile**: during the hot season tiny **fertile** cleistogamic flowers appear. This may be an effect of temperature, rather than a seasonal change.

In conclusion, we may say that the phenomenon of facultative cleistogamy appears in the nature of a biological safeguard, in that it permits some seed to be set in difficult environmental conditions which prevent the normal outbreeding mechanism, by means of cross-pollination, functioning.

CHAPTER II

THE BIOLOGY OF THE FLORAL PARTS

THE BIOLOGY OF THE CALYX

The biology of the calyx depends on its role in the biology of the flower as a whole. We think of the calyx as being largely protective in the bud stage of the flower, but it may have protective functions at other stages of the flower's life. Its structure also differs depending on what use it is put to, and we shall consider the two together.

PROTECTION OF THE FLOWER BUD

Protective calyces are usually green and "herbaceous" and in most families the sepals form a complete seal around the petals by reason of their strong imbrication in polysepalous flowers, or by contortion or imbrication combined with fusion. The valvate condition is much rarer and the parts are fused, at least at the base, as in *Vinca* and *Fuchsia*.

The length of life of a bud-protective calyx is seemingly a family characteristic. Take for instance the poppies: here, the familiar two-sepalled calyx bursts open in the early morning to release the crumpled petals and is shed forthwith, e.g. *Papaver dubium*. It is one of the shortest lived, being discarded immediately its protective function is fulfilled. In contrast to this, the calyces of the bicarpellatae, i.e. the Solanales, Personales and Lamiales are markedly persistent and are usually still found intact even when the fruits are ripe as in *Lithospermum purpurocaeruleum* (Blue Gromwell), *Myosotis* (Forget-me-not), *Solanum lycopersicum* (Tomato) and *Physalis peruvianum* (Cape

Gooseberry). The sepals of the last-mentioned plant close tightly to form the orange-coloured papery "lantern" inside which is the berried fruit. *Myosotis* sepals tend to incurve over the nutlets, but the potatoes' and foxgloves' are spread and dwarfed by the fruit.

Fig. 7. *Plumbago rosea*. Slender long tubed flat topped corolla held nearly erect and protected at the base by symsepalous calyx whose sticky glands prevent insects crawling up tube. Butterfly flower type. ×2. Average amount nectar per flower 3 mg, 21·5 per cent sugar.

PROTECTION OF THE COROLLA

Many calyces have a very important part to play in the protection of the flower *during the flowering stage*. Flowers with nectar deep seated at the bottom of the corolla tubes, although finely specialized for pollination by the highest insect classes, the bumble-bees and the carpenter-bees, have an "Achilles heel" in that the texture of the corolla is delicate and easily pierced by the mouthparts of robber bees. Thus, a gamosepalous calyx may be of great value in preventing thieving by these insects which is so detrimental to pollination. Members of the Plumbaginaceae, e.g. *Plumbago capensis* and *P. rosea* (Fig. 7), *Limonium* and *Armeria* show good examples of this kind of calyx. Yet another feature is seen in the two latter genera, for here the calyx is, in addition, scarious and tough and, moreover, has a second function of attraction as it is often brightly coloured yellow, white, pink and purple. The *Plumbago* calyx is also protective in a second way; its stalked glands trapping robbers approaching by way of the stem. The viscid calyces of *Nicotiana affinis* and *Silene anglica* act in a similar way.

FORMATION OF THE COROLLA TUBE

The gamosepalous calyx of the Silenoidae, the pinks and campions, of the Caryophyllaceae, is effective in preventing robbing of the nectar, but again has another important function, that of preserving the imbrication of the clawed petals and of holding them erect, and close together, so that they form a "tube", although they are unjoined. This calyx is also retained in the fruiting stage and so performs no less than four different duties, three protective and one of support, in its long life.

Another example similar to the one just quoted is realized by **polysepalous** calyces in the long-flowered Crucifers. Here too, the petals are long-clawed and separate, e.g. *Lunaria*, *Cheiranthus*, *Hesperis*, but the very strong imbrication of the four sepals forms and preserves the flower tube as well as protecting the nectar. Although in these cases the sepals part and are shed after anther dehiscence is completed, the flower shape is often maintained long enough to enable legitimate exploitation by long-tongued insects to take place.

THE CALYX AS A "COROLLA"

The calyx may function as the attractive whorl of the flower. This is often the case when the petals themselves are transformed into nectaries, as in *Helleborus corsicus* (Fig. 8), *Nigella* (Love-in-the-mist) and *Delphinium*, or when the petals are reduced in size or absent as in *Daphne*, *Elaeagnus* (Oleaster) and *Caltha* (Marsh Marigold). *Fuchsia* (Fig. 9a and b), however, has both attractive sepals and petals.

When functioning as a corolla, the biology of the calyx will

15

often reflect this function; that is to say, it will have a life similar to that of the petals. In very many flowers, the petals are ephemeral, their life often terminating at the end of anther dehiscence or, in certain cases which will be mentioned later,

FIG. 8. *Helleborus corsicus*, flower in advanced stage with many stamens shed, leaving axis bare, and stigmas already discoloured and dead. The tubed nectiferous petals, arranged in a ring below the abscissed stamens, remain until anther dehiscence is complete and then absciss: the coloured sepals remain. ×2.

possibly being actively terminated when pollination has occurred. Petaloid sepals have a similar fate; in *Caltha* and *Anemone* they usually stay until after the stamens have all dehisced, then they shed rapidly. In *Anemone* they have an additional protective role of closing in the afternoon and re-opening next morning. They are influenced in a similar way as are petals by the weather conditions, remaining closed if it is raining or dull, opening widely in sunshine. In the young flower their movements are precise; they open widely and close tightly. As the flower ages, their movements become less definite and, towards the end of

FIG. 9a. *Fuchsia*. Young flower with stigma receptive before anther dehiscence. The coloured calyx forms the flower tube. Within it the four strongly imbricate petals further deepen the tube. ×0·7.

their life, they remain permanently spread. This behaviour exactly parallels that of *Papaver orientalis* petals.

The *Helleborus* calyx is unusual in that it is, at first, herbaceous and protective, then becomes coloured and attractive; then, as the follicles begin to ripen, it becomes herbaceous once again. It is persistent, dying only when the stem itself dies.

The calyx tubes of some of the Daphnes and Pimeleas simulate the gamopetalous corolla to a remarkable degree, for not only are they coloured and of a similar shape and texture to the petals, but they are also strongly scented and bear the stamens attached to their tube just as in petalled flowers. This is probably the most complete "take-over" of form and function to be exhibited by the calyx which, however, still retains its protective duty in

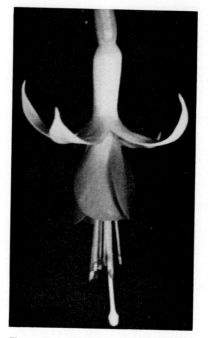

FIG. 9b. *Fuchsia.* Older flower, calyx reflexed and anther dehiscence complete. ×0·9.

the bud stage. The petaloid tube is abscissed, as is a sympetalous corolla, on completion of its corolla function, but in *Elaeagnus* the abscission takes place at the constriction in the tube, and a cup of sepal tissue remains around the ovary to perform a final protective duty. We may note that different parts of the self-same sepals have here different functions and lives.

The calyx of *Fuchsia* again plays several roles. It is protective in the bud stage, it supplements the attractive petals with its brilliant colouring, it is tubed at the base and thick in texture and so acts as a safe reservoir for the nectar. Its life terminates with that of the petals, they are abscissed together from the top of the inferior ovary (Fig. 9).

The curious "dutchman's pipe" flowers of *Aristolochia elegans* (Fig. 10) are again fashioned solely of sepals. The flare

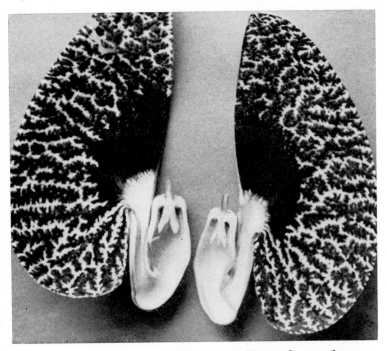

FIG. 10. *Aristolochia elegans*, Dutchman's Pipe, a fly trap flower. Calyx slit open to show the narrow neck of trap and essential organs at the base of the chamber. ×0·9.

of the sepals is blotched violet-black on a whitish ground. The colour is intensified at the mouth of the tubed part of the calyx which is flask-shaped at the base where the anthers and stigmas are situated. The chief roles of the calyx in this instance are, firstly, attraction, by reason of its foetid smell, and secondly, retention of the insect visitors involved in pollination. The

19

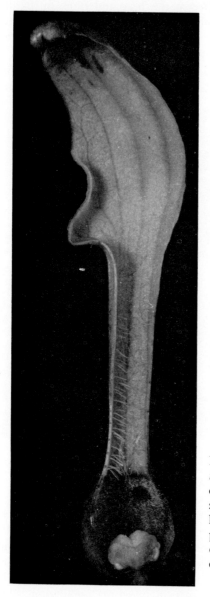

FIG. 11. *Aristolochia clematitis*, a fly-trap flower. Flower cut open to show the slide zone and downward inclined hairs in the calyx tube; with prison chamber at the base, containing the flat lobed mass of the fused stigmas and anthers. ×5·25.

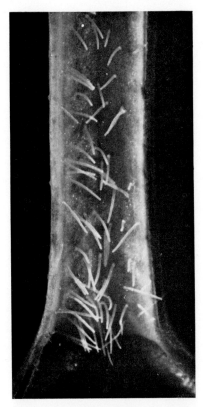

FIG. 12a. *Aristolochia clematitis.* Part of the calyx tube showing the "eel-trap" hairs with their excentric boss (an enlarged cell), preventing upward deflection beyond the horizontal which keeps the midges imprisoned in the bulbous base. × 10.

contrast pattern afforded to the insect's eye may aid in guiding it towards the mouth of the tube). The latter function devolves, in *Aristolochia clematitis* (Fig. 11), on the amazing "eel-trap" hairs which line the tube, so that the entry of insects is facilitated and their exit barred (see under Fly Flowers, and Fig. 12). The biology of the hairs is linked with that of the anthers, for they wither after the shedding of the pollen and permit egress of the potential cross-pollinators.

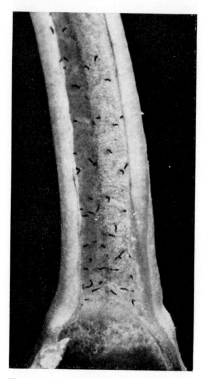

FIG. 12b. *Aristolochia clematitis.* Tube of older flower. The hairs have withered and the whole flower bends down permitting the insects, dusted with pollen, to escape. × 10.

It is difficult to assess the biological significance of the form of the calyx of *Aristolochia brasiliensis* var. *macrophylla,* which is described in the Royal Horticultural Society's *Dictionary* of *Gardening* as resembling "the head of a hawk, the beak of a heron and the wattles of a Spanish fowl"!

THE CALYX AS A NECTARY

Sepal nectaries will be mentioned under extra-floral nectaries and a few examples will be given there (Chapter V). This role of the sepal is relegated, in the Malvaceae, to the base of the sepal, the nectary being in the form of a ring or discrete spots of tissue. The sepal's chief function—that of protection—is not usurped but augmented to the production and protection of the nectar. The secretory role begins with anthesis in *Lavatera olbia* and *Abutilon striatum*. There are no data yet to hand as to its termination. In these two species the calyx lives on into the fruiting stage.

In *Thunbergia grandiflora* there is a complete transformation of the calyx into a nectary. Here, according to Pijl (1954), the identity of the sepals is lost and the calyx is just a pale-coloured ring of secreting tissue. No biological details were mentioned.

THE BIOLOGY OF THE COROLLA

Petals are the distinguishing mark of a flower to the layman, and yet they are not an essential part of it. They are inconspicuous or absent in many anemophilous flowers, and are the foremost feature of entomophilous and ornithophilous ones. They have many attributes and perform several functions.

Petals and stamens have a somewhat similar nature and biology. They are both ephemeral organs, usually non-herbaceous, and generally more delicately textured than sepals or carpels. In many flowers intermediate stages will be found between the two; petals bearing a pollen sac or petaloid stamens may be seen very commonly in the Rosaceae, particularly in the hawthorn, *Crataegus monogyna*.

ROLE AS AN ATTRACTIVE ORGAN

The chief role of the petals is the "attraction" of pollinators. All their positive attributes of scent, colour and shape are associated with this. Their biology is geared to that of the essential organs, so that they are at the height of their powers when these are mature. They are fully expanded, exude their strongest scent, and produce most of their nectar just at anther dehiscence and when the stigmas are receptive. If a flower is not pollinated, the petals will live longer, sometimes after all the stamens have died; but, once a stigma receives compatible pollen, the petals are usually shed very shortly afterwards. The most striking examples of this link occur in the orchids, where the flower life may be prolonged up to 80 days in *Oncidium*, *Cymbidium* and *Cypripedium*, if pollination does not occur. The extent of pollination of *Orobanche hederae* may be judged at a glance, weeks after flowering, by the number of dry brown corollas remaining on the spikes. They are thrown off and replaced by the swelling capsules in pollinated flowers.

Petals are variously formed and arranged for display. The simplest are obicular, equal in size and shape, unjoined and imbricated to form a shallow cup as in the actinomorphic, chasmogamic buttercups, roses and poppies. They usually have a diurnal rhythmic movement, closing over the essential organs in the afternoon and opening again next morning. These movements are most decisive, rapid and complete when the flower is young, then they become wavering and uncertain and the petals often reflex strongly shortly before they fall (e.g. *Galanthus*, *Rubus*, and *Pyrus*).

Many higher plant orders have fused petals, the bases often narrowed into a tube. Zygomorphy and epipetaly of the stamens frequently accompanies this change as in the Lamiales and Personales. Here, too, the petals seldom move once the flower has expanded, but remain permanently in positions which ensure the protection of the pollen and stigma (the significance of zygomorphy will be discussed later in connection with the flower visitors). *Nicotiana affinis* petals, however, collapse and lose their scent within 5–10 min of bright light impinging on them, leaving the stigmas unprotected and the pollen at the mercy of the Syrphids until the evening when turgor and scent return. *Matthiola bicornis* petals shrivel over the flower centre during the day. Other nocturnal flowers such as *Lonicera* and *Gladiolus* remain open, but are scented only at night. (The rhythm of scent production is largely unexplored.) In papilionaceous flowers, after the opening movement, the relative position of standard, wings and keel are maintained until the flower is tripped, after which it closes. The rate of closure of *Ulex europaeus* depends on the temperature: at 6–8°C clamping down of the standard takes 20–30 hr; at 11·2–18·3°C, 13·7 per cent of the flowers shut in 2–5 hr and 53 per cent in 10 hr. Should flowers remain unpollinated for some days the standard is gradually lowered in *Ulex*: mark, however, that the petals are retained. The biological significance of this will be demonstrated in Chapter X. Strains of Alfalfa, cultured under glass, become "trigger happy" and the flowers spring automatically making pollination studies difficult. The sides of the standard of *Trifolium repens* pinch together a little in the afternoon. If it rains overnight, frequently a drop of water lodges between them and prevents the opening movement next morning until it is dispersed. Some corollas exhibit rapid closing and opening movements. *Gentiana nivalis* will close if a cloud passes over the sun; moreover, the movement can be repeated several times. Tulips and crocuses are also sensitive and Wood (1952) has shown that the movements here are due to thermonasty. The mesophyll cells, underlying the upper surface of the tepal, grow rapidly if warmed and the tepal (perianth member) spreads outwards. When cooled, the *outer* (lower) surface mesophyll grows quickly, the tepal moves inwards, and the flower closes. Pfeffer states that crocus is sensitive to as little as 0·5°C rise in temperature. It is possible to keep the flowers just below their critical temperature so that they never open. Böhner (1934) induced a similar "cleistogamy" in tulip by the same means. The biological implications of petal movements have not been worked out.

The colour of petals is usually present when the flower is in full bud, and most brilliant when the petals first reach their maximum expansion. White is the most common colour, and this is not the easiest one for insects to remember, but yellow, blue and violet are within the colour range of the higher insects, and red can be seen by birds (see Chapters VI and IX).

Colour change with age occurs in currants, roses and *Weigelia*: generally the colour deepens from white to rose and red. *Victoria amazonica*, whose large, fragrant flowers only live for 24 hr, change from white to purplish red during this period. In

Ipomoea caerulea (Morning Glory) the ephemeral petals change from blue in the morning to pink in the afternoon, as the anthocyanin pigment in the cell sap, which is a natural indicator, reflects a change in reaction from alkaline to acid. The significance of these changes in flower colour in relation to insect visitors, has not, so far, been investigated.

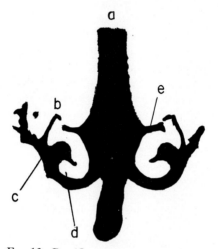

FIG. 13. *Passiflora caerulea*. Section of corolla base. a. Androgynophore, b. innermost coronal fringe whose incurved tips press against a. c. Flange, shaped like a birds' head in section, which arches over d, the nectar channel. e. Flange of fleshy protuberances which virtually close the nectar channel. × 2·25

CORONAS

The corolla may have additional appendages which are all classed together as "coronas". These are very varied in form and function and, generally speaking, are fully formed when the corolla opens and are the last part of it to wither. The coronal "trumpet" of the daffodil increases the length of the perianth tube; the "pheasant's eye" of *Narcissus poeticus* is a scent guide (see Chapter IX); coronas in the form of small scales, tufts of hairs or pouches narrow the mouth of the corolla tube in many of the Boraginaceae. The yellow corona of *Myosotis* against the blue petals furnishes a recognizable contrast for the eye of the honey-bee. The passion flowers have coronas of up to five rings of bright banded fringes: the outer are said to harbour

FIG. 14. *Asclepias tuberosa*. The coronal cups, with horn like process, secrete abundant nectar. The gland attached to the pollinia is seen as a black spot. Below is the vertical slit between the anthers leading to the receptive stigma within. × 3·25.

insects and attract the nectar birds; the inner arch over the nectar chamber (Fig. 13) and are so strong that they effectively exclude useless visitors. The corona of the Asclepiads has the double function of attraction and of secreting nectar. In *Asclepias tuberosa* (Fig. 14) it is composed of five orange cups which may brim with nectar containing 15–37 per cent sugar.

THE PETAL AS A NECTARY

The main forms of petal nectaries are described in Chapter V and while the nectar tissue is very limited in extent, the degree of modification of the petal to contain and protect it is sometimes extreme. The hellebores' tubed nectaries no longer resemble petals (Fig. 8). While remaining essentially attractive in their offer of concentrated nectar, they are without scent, which is probably disadvantageous especially as their petaloid sepals are also scentless. In February the insignificant apetalous flowers

FIG. 15. *Sarcococca ruscifolia.* Monoecious fascicle of male and female flowers. The filaments of the stamens are fragrant. × 3.

of *Sarcococca ruscifolia* with their scented stamens (Fig. 15) attract innumerable bees, while the hellebores, which have so much more to offer in nectar and pollen, are often not discovered.

THE COROLLA AS A NECTAR RESERVOIR

The texture of the petals has an important bearing on their effectiveness as a storehouse for the nectar. Many of the tube corollas, as those of *Erica cinerea* and *Trifolium pratense*, are far too delicate and thin to withstand the jaws, or even the tongues, of the stronger bumble-bees. This inherent weakness may greatly lessen the pollination potential of the species. Many flowers whose nectar is exploited by birds and Carpenter bees (*Xylocopa*), although usually more stoutly built, often suffer damage from their visitors. No critical assessment of the biological hazards is to hand. Were it not for the protection afforded by the calyx, many butterflies would find little food in the long thin tubes which appear to be so convenient for their stiletto-like tongues.

THE COROLLA AS AN AID IN POLLINATION

This will be discussed later, together with the animals involved. There are two instances, unconnected with the visits of pollinators, which may, however, be mentioned. When the corolla abscisses in some rhododendrons, it slides down the stiff filaments of the stamens with their porose anthers, and may drag pollen from them and bring it into contact with the stigma. The stigma protrudes from the corolla of the young flower of *Myosotis discolor* Pers, while the anthers are contained below in the tube. As the flower ages, the corolla tube elongates and brings the anthers level with the stigma. As dehiscence is introrse, autogamy may result. The corolla may also aid in pollination by raindrops (see Chapter III).

FUNCTION AS AN OPENING MECHANISM

Grass flowers are protected by two glumes. The lower one is strongly concave and the upper one is flattened against it so that it, too, becomes concave. Between the two lie the stamens, ovary and the lodicules. These last are thought to be the remnants of the perianth inherited from the lily ancestors, and are slender columns of colourless parenchyma. At flowering their bases become greatly swollen and exert pressure on the enfolding glumes, dislocate them, and permit the anthers and stigmas to be displayed (Fig. 16).

THE BIOLOGY OF THE ANDROECIUM

The function of the androecium is to produce and present the pollen. The methods of presentation, its rhythms and ecology are dealt with in Chapter IV.

The androecium, generally speaking, has a shorter life span than any of the other floral parts. The longevity of the androecium tends to be a family character. Most poppies are short lived; for example, *Papaver dubium*, whose petals and stamens open at 6 a.m., fall by noon. The period of anther dehiscence

FIG. 16. *Helictotrichon pubescens*, Hairy Oat Grass. The two swollen lodicules have forced the glumes apart to expose the two feathery styles. (Lower glume l.g. has been dislocated to show lodicules "in its axil" more clearly.) ×7·7.

in many grass flowers is momentary, the pollen pouring away "like peas out of a stocking" as it has been described. The Ranunculaceae have long-lived androecia. Anther dehiscence in anemones takes 7–14 days; in buttercups 2–9 days; in aquilegias 1–6 days; while the spiralled stamens of *Helleborus orientalis* dehisce in slow succession over a period of up to 26 days.

Stamens are produced lower down on the floral axis than the carpels and usually mature first. The flower is then said to be **protandrous**, as are many composites and mallows. **Protogynous** flowers, in which the stigmas mature first, are not so common. Examples are the hellebores and the hermaphrodite flowers of *Aesculus hippocastanum*, the Horse Chestnut. In buttercups, stigmas and stamens mature at about the same time and are termed **homogamous**. The two former cases constitute **dichogamy**. This condition adds a *time* factor to the space barrier between the essential organs and often nearly affects the pollination potential. Movements of stamens often play an important role in the biology of the flowers.

NATURAL MOVEMENTS

In the fully-developed, unopened bud of *Cardamine pratensis*, the Milk Maid, the long stamens are in two opposite pairs with the anthers facing one another. As the flower opens they twist outwards and dehisce extrorsely. The short stamens dehisce introrsely. The whole length of the anthers of both long and short stamens is above the level of the corolla. This means that the face of any insect probing for nectar lying at the base of the short stamens, must receive pollen on all sides. Each flower of *Tropaeolum majus*, the Garden Nasturtium, has eight anthers which are erected by the filaments, one by one, to about the centre of the flower before dehiscence. This position is maintained until after dehiscence when the filament bends away from the centre. The whole process takes from 27 to 122 hr depending on the weather. When the flower of *Reseda odorata*, the Mignonette, is "in bud", that is, before the three top petals erect themselves, the stamens are evenly disposed about the ovary. Within a day of the raising of the petals, all the stamens become strongly deflexed below the ovary. As an anther ripens it is raised before the honey disc and dehisces extrorsely in this position. This is so for 51 per cent; 34·6 per cent are raised only to the level of the ovary; 13·2 per cent dehisce *below* it and 0·5 per cent are abortive. The duration of anther dehiscence is from 3 to 8 days. In both these species the movements of the stamens ensure that fresh pollen is presented directly in the path of an insect probing for nectar throughout the flower's whole life.

The position of the stamens relative to the stigmas often changes during the flower's life. The young flower of *Clerodendrum thomsonae* has both style and stamens stretched out level before the petals; then the style bends down and the anthers dehisce (Fig. 17). The filaments then curve down and

FIG. 17. *Clerodendrum thomsonae,* Verbenaceae. Young flower with dehisced anthers held in front of the flower in line with the corolla tube. Style bent down, stigmas closed. ×2.

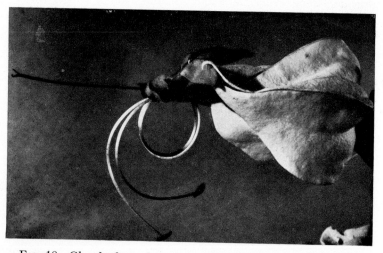

FIG. 18. *Clerodendrum thomsonae.* Older flower. Stamens curled down and style erected in line with mouth of tube with stigmas open and receptive. ×2.

finally corkscrew up while the style regains its level position and the stigmas open (Fig. 18). These movements ensure cross-pollination. The retraction of the filaments to stigma level in *Cobaea scandens*, just before the corolla falls, may effect self-pollination.

Fig. 19. *Berberis*, petal removed to show stamens with "dog eared" anthers after recovery from stimulation. Note *own* pollen is deposited just below receptive stigmatic disc. × 12.

Stimulated movements of stamens are not uncommon and, as they are brought into play by the flower visitor, may be interpreted as aids to pollination.

The barberry stamen lies back against its petal. The upper surface of the base of the filament is sensitive and, within 1/10 sec of being touched, moves inwards, so that the anther's raised "dog-ear" flaps with their pollen just touch the lower rim of the stigma (Fig. 19). Different species vary in the rapidity and

TABLE 1. Sensitivity of stamen filaments of Berberis

	Duration of inward movement of filament on 1st stimulation (Average of 30 flowers)	Recovery time after 1st stimulation	Duration of inward movement on 2nd stimulation	Recovery time after 2nd stimulation	Temperature °C.	% Relative humidity
Mahonia japonica	instantaneous	11 min		15 min	8	100
M. aquifolium	instantaneous	13 sec	1·8 sec	4 min	20·5	57
Berberis antoniana	instantaneous	12 sec			14	75
B. stenophylla	instantaneous	12 sec			20·5	53
B. darwinii	instantaneous	10 sec	0·75		14	75

extent of recovery. In *Mahonia japonica* and *M. aquifolium*, the filament recovers to the erect position only, but in *Berberis antoniana*, *B. stenophylla* and *B. darwinii*, it regains its original position back against the petal. The filaments can be stimulated for a second time, but the action is now slower, the inward movement taking 0·75–1·8 sec and the outward 4–15 min, as compared with 10 sec–11 min for the first recovery (Table 1).

Fig. 20a. *Centaurea montana*, Bumble-bee Flower. The flower form is here achieved by an inflorescence; its broken outline is particularly attractive to bees. ×0·6.

Many composites also have sensitive filaments, any one of which may contract if touched. This has two consequences: firstly, a little more pollen comes out of the anther box and, secondly, the box is tilted towards the shortened filament and may come into contact with the insect responsible for the stimulus. The effect of contraction of the filaments on pollen presentation has been investigated in *Centaurea montana* (Fig. 20). At 8 a.m., forty-eight florets, which were erect but had not begun to present pollen, were brushed across once with a needle at 10-min intervals for 2 hr and the pollen obtained was weighed.

Twenty-five per cent of the total pollen was presented on the first stimulation, roughly 10 per cent on each of the second to fourth stimulations, and 4 per cent on each of the fifth to ninth stimulations. The next five stimulations yielded only 8 per cent of the total pollen and they were discontinued. In the evening the remaining pollen which had been presented amounted to 17 per cent; this was due to the growth of the style and stigma through the anther box.

FIG. 20b. *Centaurea montana*, Early stage in pollen presentation with the style still within the strong curved anther box. ×3·8.

Layia elegans has very sensitive filaments; if one blows on the current day's ring of florets, the five filaments of each floret will shorten in turn, causing each anther box to circle and curtsey. The latter movement results in more pollen being presented. The filaments of *Centaurea nigra* were found to lose their power to react to stimulus on hot dry days (28–31°C). This seemed to be due to loss of turgor.

STAMENS AS NECTARIES

The androecium may have the double function of providing both pollen and nectar. If a stamen becomes nectar-secreting, it usually forfeits its power to produce pollen. This happens in *Anemone pulsatilla* where the anthers of the outermost stamens secrete nectar. Three of the six stamens of *Commelina coelestis* are completely sterile, the anthers being transformed into flat, four-lobed nectaries still erect on the slender filaments. The three fertile anthers dehisce directly in front of them, ensuring pollen transference if the flower is visited.

Partial sterilization of the androecium to form false nectaries is seen in *Parnassia palustris*. Each flattened staminode bears terminally nine or ten stalked shining yellow knobs. Despite their appearance, they are dry and nectarless.

PROTECTION OF THE NECTAR

This function may devolve on the filament. The bases of the five filaments of the campanulas are broadened and contiguous, and completely cover the nectar disc protecting it from small

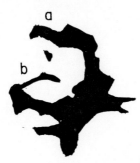

FIG. 21. *Momordica balsamina.*
L.S. flower centre. a. Central platform formed by contiguous filaments of the fertile stamens. b.
Staminode in form of a flap roofing
over the nectary. × 4.

intruders and virtually forcing a vertical probing of the column formed by them in the *young* stage of the flower. In the female flower of *Luffa cylindrica*, the broad hairy filaments of the abortive stamens largely cover the nectary. The male flower of *Momordica balsamina* has three fertile stamens with stout erect filaments, which are contiguous over the centre of the flower. Their anther lobes, separated into four branches, dehisce out-wards and downwards, the filaments themselves making a central landing platform. At *petal level*, two staminodes, each in the form of a flap, are bent over the centre of the flower virtually roofing in the nectary and leaving a single narrow opening for the visitor's tongue (Fig. 21).

THE ANDROECIUM AS AN ATTRACTIVE ORGAN

To function so, the androecium assumes in some measure the attributes of the corolla in its form, colour and scent. Possibly the most famous examples occur in the Myrtaceae. The thick brushes of stamens, which erect themselves in the *Eucalyptus* flower when the cap of petals is thrown off, form a cup-like

FIG. 22. *Acacia* sp. Two inflorescences of tight massed flowers with brushes of long yellow scented stamens and styles projecting beyond them. × 2·4.

" corolla " and may be any shade from white in the Snow Gum (*Eucalyptus coriacea*), to vivid scarlet in the Red Gum (*Eucalyptus ficifolia*). In the Callistemons (the Pink and Red Bottle Brushes), *Metrosideros* (the Scarlet Rata) and *Melaleuca* (the Paper Bark), only the stamens are attractive. These genera have but little scent in contrast to the acacias, the wattles. Here the " powder puff " capitula are strongly scented, the filaments again forming the attractive fluff (Fig. 22).

The erect, stout, close set filaments of the swamp grapefruit (*Citrus* sp.) form a "corolla" within the petals, converting the flower from a shallow to a deep form (Fig. 23). The false corona of *Eucharis grandiflora* (Fig. 24) is composed of the broad contiguous bases of the filaments, the anthers standing above. Viewed under ultra-violet light the dehisced anthers glow like

FIG. 23. *Citrus*, Orange Blossom. The broad contiguous filaments of the stamens form a tube protecting the circular nectary at the base of the style. Anther dehiscence is complete and the broad flattened stigma sticky and receptive. ×8·6.

39

six brilliant white candles on a birthday cake; it is the pollen which is fluorescent.

Vogel (1954) describes a South African "stone" plant, *Conophytum*, in which a false corolla is formed out of fused staminodes which, in section, resembles very strongly the tube of a *Lychnis*, except that here the fertile anthers are fused half-way down the inside of the tube.

The insignificant apetalous flowers of the January-flowering *Sarcococca ruscifolia* (Fig. 15) are remarkable in their heavy

FIG. 24. *Eucharis grandiflora*, Amaryllidaceae. Moth flower, white, sweet scented with long curved tube and no landing platform. False corona formed by the broad bases of the stamen filaments. Nat. size.

fragrance. To find the location of the scent, the flowers were divided into their component parts and put into small corked tubes. After 15 min the tubes were sniffed in turn by thirteen humans, aged 18–50 years, and presence of scent was recorded. The results showed that the fragrance was located chiefly in the filaments:

	Scent present
Filaments + anthers	13
Anthers	9
Calyces of male flowers	1
Female flowers	6 (3 of these only "slightly")

This plant is always buzzing with bees on mild winter days.

Lastly, the androecium may attract insects by reason of the scent of the pollen alone, as in *Polygonum bistorta*, the other parts of the flower being scentless (Porsch, 1954).

THE BIOLOGY OF POLLEN

LENGTH OF LIFE

The longevity of pollen grains varies greatly between different species. That of the cereals is usually short-lived; indeed, Barley pollen dies if it is not transferred immediately to the stigma. At the other end of the scale is the Date Palm, *Phoenix dactylifera*, whose pollen will live for a year. McGregor Skene (1932) gives the following data on viability:

Hibiscus trionum	3 days
Trifolium	12 days
Paeonia	8 weeks
Narcissus poeticus	10 weeks
Apple	3 months

GERMINATION OF POLLEN

Pollen grains may be in one of two stages when they are shed. Either they are binucleate, that is containing a tube nucleus and a generative nucleus, or they are trinucleate. In these latter, the generative nucleus has divided to form two sperms. The binucleate pollen germinates freely in sugar solutions, water or gelatine. *Caladium* pollen germinates well if merely damped, in 5–6 hr. This kind of pollen may often germinate on foreign stigmas; whether fertilization follows, depends on the closeness of the taxonomic relationship between the plants. The concentration of sugar required for germination varies from 3–5 per cent for *Allium ursinum*, up to 70 per cent for *Cassia*. Many bee- and bird-pollinated flowers belonging to the Rosaceae, Liliaceae and Solanaceae have binucleate pollen.

Trinucleate pollen will seldom germinate except on a compatible stigma. The Composites and grasses have this type of pollen. Sometimes the conditions necessary for germination are very precise. Larsen and Tung (1950) working with Danish varieties of apple found that both pH and sugar concentration affected germination; for example 30 per cent sucrose at pH 4·9 supported better germination than 21·5 per cent sucrose at pH 6·9. Ericaceous pollen requires an acid solution for germination and, experimentally, malic acid proved the most effective. Sometimes the presence of substances excreted by the stigma are essential. *Forsythia intermedia* flowers are heterostylous and self-sterile. Moewus (1950) found that the pollen from the short-styled flower contains a germination inhibitor, Quercetin-3-rutinosid, and will only grow if it is placed on the long-styled flowers whose stigmas contain a rutin splitting enzyme. The pollen from the long-styled flower contains another flavone, Quercetrin. In the stigmas of the short-styled flowers alone will it find the Quercetrin splitting enzyme necessary for its growth. Another special case is that of *Oncidium flexuosum* (Orchidaceae), where the pollen is killed if it is deposited on the stigmas of the selfsame flower.

The genetic constitution of the pollen grain may affect its behaviour on the stigma. In the dioecious Red Campion, *Silene dioica*, the constitution of the female plants is XX, and of the male plants XY. The pollen grains carry either an X factor or a Y factor; the eggs only have the X factor. The pollen tubes of the X grains grow faster than the Y grains. If there are only a few male plants in the population, the insect pollinators will be likely to carry but little pollen to the female plants. There will therefore be plenty of room on the stigmas, and the X and Y pollen tubes will both be able to reach the ovules. Hence the proportion of male and female plants in the progeny will be more or less equal. If male plants predominate in the population, the stigmas are likely to receive a lot of pollen. Consequently, the fast growing X grains will crowd out the slower Y's and more female plants will be produced which will adjust the balance of the two sexes in the population.

Orchardists, wishing to secure apple pollen in bulk for hybridizing, collected pollen pellets from the hive bee but, after storage, it would not germinate. Maurizio (1958) has shown that the secretion of the pharyngeal glands of the honey-bee contains an inhibitor which prevents the germination of pollen; and honey does so too. The regurgitated liquid, which is mainly honey, with which the bee cements its load, apparently acts likewise.

SENSITIVITY OF POLLEN

The pollen of the cereals, Barley, Wheat and Rye, is extremely sensitive to drying and yet bursts immediately if it is wetted. In the two former plants this is guarded against by dehiscence and pollination before the glumes open. In many entomophilous flowers the grains have an oily coat which prevents wetting by rain.

Lidfors (1896) compared the sensitivity of pollen with the amount of protection afforded by the corolla and found that on the whole unprotected pollen is resistant to damage by water, and sensitive pollen is protected. This difference is seen in the two related genera *Rumex* and *Polygonum*. The former is anemophilous and has unprotected pollen, resistant to water: the latter is entomophilous, self-pollinated or even cleistogamous, and has sensitive protected pollen.

Effect of heat. At Timbuctu, Hagerup (1932) reports that the air is so hot and dry (40–45°C at about 2 m from the ground) that anemophilous pollen cannot survive more than a very brief passage by air. The plants which do succeed in being wind-pollinated are only those which have close set flowers such as *Ambrosia senegalensis* D.C. and grasses with dense panicled inflorescences.

THE BIOLOGY OF THE STIGMA AND STYLE

There is a paucity of information on the biology of the stigma. The essential functions of it are the capture of pollen grains and the provision of a suitable surface on which they may germinate.

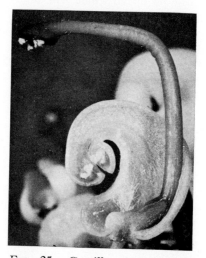

FIG. 25. *Grevillea rosmarinifolia*, Proteaceae. Bird-pollinated. Vertical section. Note flowers' own pollen from protandrous episepalous anthers adhering to stylar plate. The nectary and large nectar drop is at the base of the pouched scarlet calyx which functions as a corolla. × 3·5.

This is only possible during a limited period when it is damp or sticky (Fig. 23), when it is said to be **receptive**. Before and after this the pollen will not stick to it. A casual inspection of the broad, flat stigma of *Grevillea rosmarinifolia* would seem to disprove this, as it bears pollen with which it came into contact in the bud stage (Figs. 25 and 26). However the real stigma is a central point of tissue which matures later, and the pollen is

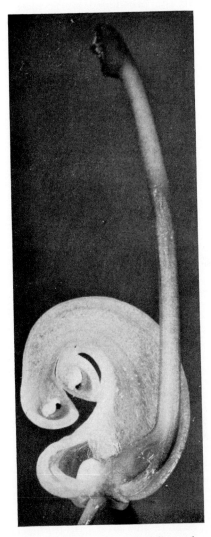

FIG. 26. *Grevillea rosmarinifolia,* style erect.
Note pinpoint stigma, free of pollen in the
centre of plate to which latter some pollen still
adheres. ×4·25.

adhering only to the broadened stylar plate. This pollen is largely removed by the bird visitors and used in cross-pollination: it does, however, give a chance of autogamy at a later stage, if any of it remains. The secretion which renders the stigma sticky varies in amount. In apples, pears, and stone fruits a

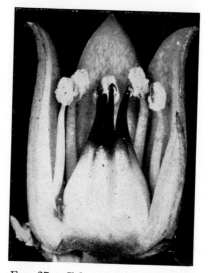

Fig. 27a. *Echeveria retusa hybrida*, Crassulaceae. Flower in anthesis and with a bead of nectar oozing from each stigma. ×3·6.

slight moistness is all that is discernible. In the Magnolias and the Black Poplar, it may attract insect pollinators, as in both these plants the fluid oozing out is quite abundant and sweet. The stigmas of *Echeveria retusa hybrida* also produce large drops of nectar (Fig. 27) and so too does each female flower of *Arum maculatum* (Fig. 28). In the latter case the nectar may serve as refreshment for the imprisoned gnats. Even in the minute *Wolffia arrhiza*, whose whole plant body is but 1–1·5 mm in width, the female flower, which is a single carpel, produces a "pollination drop" which is renewed if it is wiped away (McCann,

1942). The male flower, a single stamen, dehisces first and the pollen is probably conveyed to the stigma by tiny insects crawling over the close masses of floating fronds.

Musa textilis, the Manilla Hemp, is nocturnal, the buds opening in the late afternoon when the stigmas of the female and

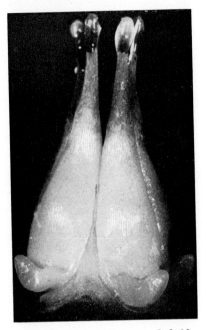

Fig. 27b. *Echeveria retusa hybrida*, Crassulaceae. Ovaries with crescent shaped nectaries at base. ×7.

hermaphrodite flowers immediately become receptive by extruding a white sticky mucilage. They remain receptive for 2 days, but successful pollination can only occur at night or in the early morning, as the stigmatic secretion becomes hard in the afternoon and pollen will not stick to it. As the stigma ages it gradually loses its receptivity and its colour changes from yellowish white to blue: its tissues also become more acid altering from pH 6 to pH 4–5 (Nur, 1958).

Fig. 28. *Arum maculatum* inflorescence. Fly-trap "flower".
At base of spathe note female
flowers in receptive stage with
nectar drop on the stigmas of two,
above them a few sterile flowers,
then the male flowers in anthesis
and, at the top, sterile flowers with
long processes. Two abnormal
female flowers are seen at bottom
left. × 3·3.

For the most part the capture of the pollen is passive, it has
to be transferred to the stigma by the pollinator, and, if it does
not soon germinate, it may be brushed off again by wind, rain
or another visitor. In *Verbascum* and *Acanthus*, the stigma
plays a more active role. In both these genera it is like a valve,
opening only when it is receptive and closing again shortly after

pollen is deposited upon it. Much the same thing happens in *Pavonia rosea*. The stigma has a circular fringe of hairs and these close in tightly over the pollen grains. *Mimulus* shows a higher degree of efficiency, for here the valves of the stigma are sensitive, and close rapidly when touched, opening again if pollination has not occurred. They are able to perform this movement several times. The receptive stigma exercises a considerable influence on the growth of the pollen tubes, often favouring that of the grains from another flower above that of its own pollen. This is the case in **heterostylic** flowers. A classic example is the primrose, *Primula vulgaris*, with its long styled "pin-eyed" flowers and short styled "thrum-eyed" flowers. These are borne on separate plants. The stigmas are also dimorphic: the papillae of the receptive surface in the pin-eyed flowers are three times as long as those of the thrum-eyed. The pollen is of two sizes: the grains of the thrum-eyed flowers are half as large again as those of the short stamens of the pin-eyed. Cross-pollination of the two types of flower is necessary for seed set, i.e. when the large pollen is placed on the stigma with the long papillae, and vice versa. The exact nature of barrier to successful self-pollination is not known.

In *Lythrum salicaria*, the Loosestrife, the styles, the stigmas, the stamen filaments, the pollen grains and the flowers themselves, are all trimorphic. Individual plants have only one type of flower. The long-styled flower has one ring of short and one ring of medium length stamens; the mid-styled one ring of long and one of short stamens, and the short-styled one ring of long and one of medium length stamens (Fig. 29). The stigmatic papillae average 166, 132, and 81 μ in length in the long-, mid- and short-styled flowers respectively.

The diameter of the pollen grains is 33, 24, and 20 μ in the long, mid and short stamens respectively. The long-styled flower, with the longest and most widely separated stigmatic papillae is most successfully pollinated by the large green pollen grains of the long stamens. The short and medium length stamens have yellow small grained pollen which germinates on the close set and shorter papillae of the short- and mid-styled flowers respectively. As in the primrose, the most successful pollination and subsequent seed set is between pollen grains and stigmas which are matched in size; but the exact nature of the stigmatic influence on pollen germination is unexplained.

Moewus (1950) has shown that the incompatibility factors in the stigma and pollen of the heterostylous *Forsythia intermedia* are physiological and biochemical (*see* Biology of Pollen). The

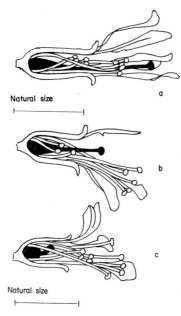

Natural size

a

b

c

Natural size

Fig. 29. *Lythrum salicaria*. Species with trimorphic flowers: a. long-styled, b. mid-styled, c. short-styled. × 3–3·5.

style is not an essential organ. It is absent in the more primitive families of the Ranunculaceae and Papaveraceae, and even the climax groups of the Cruciferae and Orchidaceae have sessile stigmas. Flowers with corolla tubes usually have styles which carry the stigmas high up in the tube or above it. In the latter case, the style not only bears the stigma, but presents it in a particular place at a particular time, so that the potentiality for cross-pollination is enhanced. In *Digitalis lanata* and *Acanthus mollis*, the style remains pressed back against the upper lobe of the corolla (Fig. 30a) (the over-arching sepal in the latter plant), for up to 7 days, during which time the anthers complete their

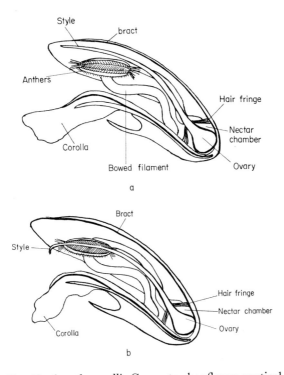

FIG. 30. *Acanthus mollis*. Carpenter-bee flower, vertical section. a. 2nd day of flowering, style above anthers, stigmas closed. Anthers have dehisced but hair fringes prevent pollen falling. Strong bowed filaments offer resistance to insects' entry. b. 7th day, style moving down, stigmas still shut. (Natural size).

dehiscence and the pollen is mostly carried away by the insect visitors (*Bombus* and *Xylocopa* respectively). Then the style begins to move downward (Fig. 30b), until it is within 2–3 mm of the lower lip, that is, right in the path of the insect. As it moves, the lobes of the stigma open and become receptive. As the insects concerned habitually work from the bottom to the top of the flower spike, this concerted action is admirably timed to secure cross-pollination. In *Clerodendrum thomsonae*, the

51

sequence of events is the same, but during anther dehiscence the style is recurved below the level of the stamens. It later moves up in front of the mouth of the corolla tube, at which time the stigmas open and the filaments of the stamens curve down, entirely preventing self-pollination.

The style of the Compositae plays a double role, firstly it presents the pollen by growing up through the anther box and pushing it out, and secondly, it carries the stigmas well above their own pollen. It is sometimes modified to perform the first task by being thickened below its tip or furnished with a ring of hairs which assist in sweeping out the pollen. The two stigmas diverge only when clear of the anther box: those of *Helianthus annuus* recurve and come in contact with their own pollen towards evening.

The style may participate actively in pollination. In Alfalfa, *Medicago sativa* and Broom, *Sarothamnus scoparius*, when the flower is tripped, the style recoils violently and hits the insect on the back of the thorax, depositing pollen and also bringing the stigma into contact with it.

CHAPTER III

AGENCIES OF POLLINATION

THE agencies of pollination fall into two groups: firstly, there are the **natural** agencies, and secondly, the **animal** agencies.

The natural agencies of pollination are wind, water and rain. Pollination by wind is termed **anemophily** and the flower is said to be **anemophilous**. Pollination by water is termed **hydrophily** and the flower is said to be **hydrophilous**. Pollination by rain has only recently been described and no term has been coined for it.

The animal agencies of pollination are insects, birds and small mammals such as bats.

Pollination by insects is termed **entomophily**, and the flowers are **entomophilous**. Pollination by birds is termed **ornithophily**, and the flowers are **ornithophilous**. Pollination by bats is termed **cheiropterophily**, and the flowers are **cheiropterophilous**.

There are some rather doubtful records of pollination by snails, termed **malacophily**, and the Aspidistra is said to be **malacophilous**.

Whichever agency is employed in pollination, the plant is usually a passive partner in the transaction. Beyond the display of its "goods for sale", the flower remains static; but, as always in biology, there are numerous exceptions to the rule. These are not entirely confined to the animal-pollinated flowers; there is the rare case of participation by the explosive discharge of pollen into the air in the anemophilous *Ricinus communis* and

Parietaria diffusa which is described elsewhere, and Jaeger (1961), citing Wettstein, describes how the whole male flower of *Mercurialis annua* is hurled from the plant by the pressure of the reflexed sepals against the main axis, which causes the delicate pedicel to fracture.

The movements of the style and stamens in the higher entomophilous metachlamydeae, by which first one and then the other is presented in a suitable position for contact with the visitor, are not infrequent. These devices lessen the probability of autogamy, or even make it impossible, and increase the chance of geitonogamy and xenogamy.

The animal is the active partner, and, in essence, its value to the plant will be determined by the extent to which it effects cross-pollination between the individuals of the plant population. The animal agents will be considered separately and their role as pollinators assessed.

ANEMOPHILY

Pollination by wind is probably the most ancient type. The plant groups which flourished in the Carboniferous and Mesozoic were chiefly vascular cryptogams and gymnosperms. The former still retain the motile sperm and are dependent on the presence of a film of water at the time of fertilization. The gymnosperms, with certain exceptions among the Gnetales, are all wind-pollinated at the present day, and were presumably so in earlier times. Pollen-feeding insects may have visited them, or, if the sporophylls were fleshy, they may have been gnawed, but it is unlikely that these insects of the primary and secondary rocks, which all have *biting* jaws, did more than exploit the "flowers" without any benefit accruing to the plant. There was however one widespread Mesozoic group, the Bennettitales, which had an arrangement of sporophylls comparable to that of the angiosperm flower. The fertile axis bore firstly rings of hairy bracts, then a circle of feathery stamens and lastly a "cone" of stalked ovules (see under Flower Form); a "set up" which could benefit from the visits of a pollen feeder.

Flowers depending on the two natural agencies of pollination, wind and water, are remarkably similar in their structure. They possess none of the positive "attractive" attributes of the entomophilous species, but are chiefly composed of the essential organs alone. The flowers of anemophilous trees are frequently arranged in "catkins" and these are usually unisexual. The male catkins are often pendulous and their axes are *flexible* so that they are easily swayed or shaken by the wind. There is more uniformity of structure among the male catkins than among the female. Those of Alder, Hazel, Birch, Poplar, Oak, She-oak (*Casuarina*) and Hornbeam are all of the "lamb's tail" kind. The female inflorescences of Birch, Alder and She-oak are *stiff* erect catkins; those of the two latter become cone-like in fruit. In all three the ovaries are hidden within the bud scales and the stigmas alone appear above their rims. Hazel is similar with a bunch of red stigmas protruding from the tip of the perulate (scaly) bud. Oak and Beech have groups of two to five minute flowers, each (occasionally two) surrounded by a cupule of fused bracts which form the cup of the acorn and the four-valved spiny involucre of the beech nut at maturity. Poplars and *Garrya elliptica* (Fig. 31) differ in that both the male *and* female catkins are pendant and flexible. In all these genera the stigmas of the ovaries are not remarkably long nor are they feathery which is contrary to expectation considering their mode of pollination. But their whole surface is, apparently, receptive, so that collectively they are presenting a considerable catchment area for pollen. The exposed tips alone of the stigmas in a single female catkin of Alder measure, collectively, some 210 mm in length. The other major anemophilous group, the Gramineae, have spreading paniculate inflorescences with wiry rhachices which move freely in the lightest air currents, and the docks (*Rumex*) also have panicles of slender pedicelled flowers.

Flowers of wind pollinated plants are freely exposed and often **precocious**, so there is no obstruction by the foliage to the free dissemination of the pollen. The grass inflorescence is raised above the level of the turf, and, although it is easily "laid" by rain and storm, has the power of re-erection by means of differential growth just above the node. The anthers, if they are not inserted on a flexible axis, are often on long slender filaments, and, in the grasses and plantains (*Plantago*), they are versatile— that is, attached midway along their length so that they swing

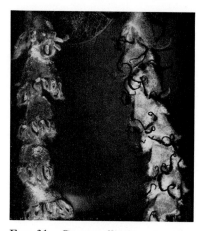

FIG. 31. *Garrya elliptica.* Anemophilous dioecious species. Both catkins have flexible axes. Left, male catkin in anthesis; right, female catkin, late stage with stigmas withered. ×2·7.

easily. This is assumed to assist in pollen dispersal, but in fact the pollen usually pours out as soon as dehiscence occurs leaving the anthers quite empty.

The pollen is smooth-coated and dry and has no oily coating, but that of *Betula* is slightly sticky. Moreover the grains are shed singly and not in tetrads as in the Ericaceae. That of *Calluna vulgaris* is an exception to the rule: the tetrads dry as the flower ages, and become wind borne. Generally speaking anemophilous plants produce far greater amounts of pollen than entomophilous species. Pohl (1937) estimates that single male plants of *Mercurialis annua* and *Rumex acetosa* produce respectively some 1,352,000,000 and 393,000,000 pollen grains.

The False Oat grass *Arrhenatherum elatius*; the Rye, *Secale cereale* and *Zea mais* produce approximately 75,000,000, 21,000,000, and 18,500,000 pollen grains per plant.

Hyde (1945), however, makes an interesting comparison between *Tilia cordata* and *Quercus petraea*. *Tilia* produces 43,000 pollen grains per flower, and *Quercus* 41,200. It is calculated that the total pollen production of a stand $100 \times 100\,\text{m}$ of the two trees over a period of 50 years would be $280,490 \times 10^6$ for *Tilia* and $34,410 \times 10^6$ for *Quercus*! Hyde's records also prove that *Tilia* pollen although of the entomophilous type, is quite abundantly air borne.

Another feature of anemophilous plants is that the flowers are individually very small and their perianths are insignificant or altogether lacking. In some cases the lack of floral envelopes is a result of reduction from entomophilous flowers, as in the wind-pollinated *Thalictrum* (Meadow Rue) among the petaloid Ranunculaceae. Another example is *Tristicha ramosissima*, an anemophilous member of the aquatic Podostemaceae (Willis, 1902). Even where the perianth is retained it has little or no colour. It is green in the nettles, and an almost transparent envelope in *Garrya elliptica* (Fig. 31). Such colour as occurs in the flower is chiefly in the anthers or the stigmas. The scarlet stigmas of *Corylus avellana* have no attraction for insects, and indeed they are probably not distinguished, as but few insects can see red.

Anemophilous flowers do not possess nectaries although the stigmas of some species e.g. *Populus nigra* exude quite large drops of sweetish fluid which remind one of the pollination drop which issues from the micropyle of gymnosperm ovules, especially in the genus *Ephedra*. There are very few ovules in the ovaries, two only in *Corylus*, *Casuarina*, *Juglans*, *Fagus* and *Quercus*, and one in *Urtica*, *Parietaria*, *Ulmus*, *Betula*, and *Myrica* (Sweet Gale) and the grasses. Is this indicative of the efficacy of wind-pollination? Rempe, on Heligoland, trapped 955 Oak pollen grains per cm^2 of a sticky surface, in $3\frac{1}{2}$ days, which would mean that the receptive stigmas of an Oak flower, whose surface area is 0.8–1 mm would receive about 10 grains in a similar period (Jaeger, 1961). This would appear to be

57

ample for the fertilization of the single ovule should the stigmas remain receptive for several days, but no data is given as to their length of life.

THE EFFICACY OF WIND-POLLINATION

In assessing this we must take into consideration not only the power of the pollen to remain airborne but also the effects of the aerial environment on its vitality.

The first aspect has been investigated over many years by Hyde (1942–1952) who has shown that 95 per cent of the pollen caught on slides 60 ft above ground in South Wales is that of wind-pollinated plants, the other 5 per cent being entomophilous pollen. The incidence of any particular species of tree pollen falls to a low figure at a distance of $\frac{1}{4}$ mile from the source. These results are very different from Rempe's data (cited by Jaeger, 1961) which prove the transport of large quantities of Pine, Oak and Birch pollen over a distance of 30 miles from the mainland to the virtually treeless island of Heligoland. The latter station may be windier. Rempe (1937) by trapping pollen on sticky slides during flights at different altitudes, proved that large quantities occurred up to 200 m. He also showed that up to 37·8 per cent of the total daily (24 hr) " catch " of pollen on the roof of the Botanical Institute at Gottingen was deposited there *during the night*, presumably from the upper air, as anemophilous plants do not release their pollen in the hours of darkness. The catch was chiefly composed of tree pollens, which is to be expected as these are shed into the environment of the macroclimate and are more likely to be carried upwards by thermals.

Hyde and Williams (1945), however, found that vertical deposition of grass pollen was not significantly greater at night, which is rather odd because they found that immediately a grass came into flower its pollen was caught in abundance at roof level. Different species of grasses come to anther dehiscence at different times of day. *Arrhenathrum elatius* flowers about 5 a.m., while *Festuca rubra* and *Holcus lanatus* flower chiefly in late afternoon. The period of anthesis is very short; there is a great burst of flowering then it stops quite as suddenly. Hyde and Williams' graphs show that the local concentration of grass pollen rose and fell with the flowering of the grasses. There was no time lag in between the two. It would appear then that grass pollen is not airborne for very long, and it may be that the gregarious habit of grasses is very necessary for their adequate pollination. We may also note that anemophilous trees and aquatics such as *Littorella* and *Potamogeton* are also gregarious.

Maize pollen is very large (90–100 μ diam.; cf. Wheat 48–57 μ) and unless a breeze is blowing it falls almost vertically to the ground. Two features of the female inflorescence, the corn "cob", mitigate this disadvantage. Firstly, the cobs are borne lower down on the stem than the terminal male panicle, and secondly, the stigmas are phenomenally long and hang in 6–9 in. tassels or "silks" from the top of the husks clasping the cob.

THE EFFECT OF THE AERIAL MEDIUM ON THE VIABILITY OF POLLEN

According to Werfft (cited Jaeger), the short ultraviolet waves are harmful to pollen, and even 8 hr exposure to sunlight killed 90 per cent of Hornbeam pollen. The long distance carriage of pollen (up to 500 miles is quoted for *Pinus*) is probably of little biological value.

Barley appears as well adapted for wind pollination as many of its sister genera, yet its seemingly perfect mechanism is obsolete. The reason is that the pollen is so sensitive to both drying and wetting that it cannot survive air transport. The anthers open before the glumes and the flowers are self-pollinated in the "bud" stage.

TAXONOMY OF WIND POLLINATED PLANTS

Modern anemophilous angiosperms belong to the **climax** groups of the rose and lily alliances. The Rosaceous line (J. Hutchinson's classification) begins to show modification in the direction of anemophily at the level of the Hamamelidales: genera such as *Parrotia*, *Sycopsis* and *Edgeworthia* have tight fasicles of apetalous flowers with attractive stamens freely exposed, in the first genus they are even precocious. Next come the willows with their male and female catkins, the flowers of which consist but of naked ovaries and paired stamens. Here, further preparation is made towards anemophily by the precocity of the flowers and the dioecism of the plants. But the last steps are not seen among the willows, for their catkins are stiff instead of being flexible, their pollen is sticky-coated instead of dry, and a nectary is present on each flower's pedicel. The nectar is abundant and quite rich, Vansell gives it as 60 per cent in America: 17–20·5 per cent is found in Wales. *Salix* is the chief early spring source of nectar and pollen for all the early bees, honey and bumble, and hosts of vernal Andrenas: despite its looks, it is truly entomophilous.

One climax group of the Rose line is the Fagales. Here at last we have the truly anemophilous genera of the oaks, beeches, birches, alders, and hornbeams whose floral characters have already been described. Even among these, one entomophilous species, *Castanea sativa*, the Sweet Chestnut, remains.

Other climax groups of the Rose stock are also anemophilous. The Casuarinas or She-oaks of Australia have articulated branches with leaves reduced to scales and bear a strong resemblance to *Equisetum*. They may be large trees or shrubs. The male catkins are pendulous, their bracts forming a series of cups from which the anthers on their delicate filaments depend. The female flowers are protected by bracts which become tough and coriaceous and actually enclose the ovaries after pollination and reopen to release the seed.

Lastly, there are the true nettles, the Urticaceae, a herbaceous family in the Ulmales. The flowers again are tiny and apetalous, but the calyx is retained and plays a part in the explosive release of the pollen into the air. The common stinging nettle, *Urtica dioica*, is dioecious.

The Gramineae is the other main anemophilous family of the Angiosperms. Again we find that it is a climax group, showing the ultimate modification and reduction from the lily flower with its six tepals and stamens and tricarpellary ovary, to three stamens and a single-seeded ovary surmounted by two feathery styles, the tepals perhaps being represented by the lodicules (Fig. 16).

Porsch (1956) notes that many bees and still more beetles visit wind-pollinated plants for pollen and suggests that this may indicate that insect pollination preceded wind pollination in the angiosperms. He also draws attention to the fact that the pollen of *Zea mais* and some species of Carex is scented, and that this is a relic of insect pollination. In the *modern* anemophilous plants this is probably so, for, according to Hutchinson (see above) they are derived from the rose and lily lines.

HYDROPHILY

Angiosperms which have returned to the haven of life in water show very different degrees of adaptation to their "new" habitat. The conservatism of the flower, which makes it such a valuable organ in taxonomy, is now exhibited in an entirely different way. Its behaviour in most aquatics is still that of a land plant. No matter how vast the modification of the vegetative body, by hook or by crook, the flowers are produced *above* the water and pollination is still either entomophilous or anemophilous. The remarkable members of the Podostemaceae which live in fast-flowing tropic streams of marked periodicity, may, in the brief period of their flowering, produce masses of tiny brilliant pink or white, *scented*, chasmogamic flowers which are pollinated by bees! (Brown, B. C., 1876) cited by Arber in *Water Plants*. The vegetative body of the plant is thalloid and resembles an alga, even to the holdfasts by which it clings to the rocky stream bed, yet when the waters subside it flowers to reveal its true nature as a derivative of the Saxifrage family. From the entomophilous flowers just mentioned, there is, in this family, a series showing progressive reduction of the flower, first, with loss of the perianth to anemophily as in *Tristicha ramosissima*, then to self-pollination as in *Lawia zeylanica*; then, strangely enough to **zygomorphy** with asymmetry of the perianth, the loss of the two upper stamens, and an unequal development of the carpels as in species of *Hydrobryum* and finally, to cleistogamy and autogamy in *Podostemon barberi*. So within one aquatic family we range through four states of flowering without the adoption of hydrophily! Zygomorphy is a feature usually associated with entomophily, but here it is not so. Willis (1901) attributes it to the dorsiventrality impressed on all parts of the plant by its growth habit. In the aquatic habitat it is of no use at all, and he speaks of the flowers which develop flat on the thallus as trying to "escape from their dorsiventrality" by curving both stamens and ovary upwards as they mature. Fortunately the pedicels, when present, are negatively geotropic, so that there is a chance of presenting the flower above water.

Other aquatic families have members whose flowers show a gradation from the attractive chasmogam presented at or above the water surface, to the totally submerged and truly aquatic flower. Such a series is exhibited by the Hydrocharitaceae. At the top, is the partly submerged *Ottelia cordata* with its attractive trimerous unisexual flowers; then follows the free floating *Hydrocharis morsus-ranae* (Frogbit) whose white petals have a basal yellow spot (a nectar guide?). Then come *Stratiotes aloides*, the Water Soldier, a submerged aquatic *which rises to the surface* at flowering time; *Vallisneria spiralis*, the Ribbon Weed, with surface flowers; and lastly, *Halophila*, a totally submerged perennial of tropical seas whose flowers have truly hydrophilous pollination.

The change to water pollination is accompanied by a disappearance of the positive attributes of scent, colour and nectar from the flower. The floral envelopes are small, often only a single whorl of sepals remaining, and in the simplest this, too, is lacking and the flower may be but a single naked ovary or stamen as in the submerged Star Worts, the Callitriches. With this simplification is an overall reduction in size and a tendency for the flower to become unisexual, and also for the plants themselves to be dioecious as in *Elodea canadensis* and *Zostera marina*. It may be noted that despite the diminution in floral parts, if the flowers are to be pollinated above water, they always reach the surface *dry*. They are completely protected by enveloping bracts or spathes for the whole of their underwater life.

As indicated above, there are different degrees of hydrophily. True hydrophily, where the pollen is water-borne, is rare and only occurs in totally submerged aquatics. The best known of these are the marine perennials, the grass wracks, *Zostera* and *Phyllospadix*, and *Halophila* which is allied to *Vallisneria*. It is only in these plants that the *pollen itself* is modified to suit the environment. *Zostera marina* has separate inflorescences of male and female flowers enclosed in the sheathing base of a grass-like leaf. The male flower is a single sessile anther. The anther wall

FIG. 32. *Zostera marina*, Hydrophilous species. Skein of pollen grains each of which is as long as the loculus. ×129.

has no endothecium as have the land plants, and when it is mature it dehisces by absorbing water which causes the innermost cells to swell and burst the sac. The pollen grains are enormously elongated and needle-like and stretch the whole length of the anther (Fig. 32). They have no exine and are shed naked into the sea. They are non-motile but coil around the stigmas of the female flower if they drift against them.

The individual pollen grains of *Halophila* are short, but they are united into thread-like strings which catch against the filiform styles; the latter may measure up to 26 mm. *Cymodocea*, a marine relative of the brackish water aquatic, *Zannichellia*, has bifid stigmas and thread-like pollen. The British *Zannichellia palustris* has globose pollen and a funnel-shaped stigma (Fig. 33). There is no information as to the significance of these paired characters for pollination.

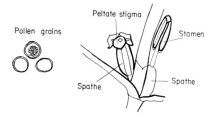

FIG. 33. *Zannichellia palustris*, Hydrophilous species. At left, a group of female flowers with peltate stigmas within a spathe: at right, spathe with male flower, a single stamen. ×5. Pollen grains large and circular.

Ceratophyllum demersum, the hornwort, has hydrophilous pollination, but is remarkable in that anther dehiscence occurs *in the air* and then the pollen returns to the water. The male flowers are axillary and consist of a fasicle of stamens surrounded by a perianth of narrow-toothed bracts. Each stamen rises separately to the surface, the broad-tipped connective acting as a float. The anther dehisces at the surface and then, as the specific gravity of the pollen is slightly greater than that of water, it sinks gently down on to the elongated bifid stigmas of the female flowers. Jaeger (1961) reports a gentle autonomous movement of the leaves which may also waft the pollen to its destination.

Specific gravity of the pollen also aids in the water pollination of some of the submerged Callitriches. Here, oil globules in the grains render them lighter than water and keep them suspended while borne by the current to the stigmas.

Other water plants show what may be termed a "surface hydrophily". *Vallisneria spiralis*, the Ribbon Weed, is dioecious. Solitary female flowers rise, enclosed in a spathe, on long, tenuous pedicels to the surface of the water where the perianth opens disclosing three bifid stigmas. The spathe embracing the male flowers opens and they are released separately and float to the surface, aided by a bubble of air imprisoned in their sepals. No less than two thousand male flowers, each with two or three stamens may be found in each spathe. Arriving at the surface, Scott (1869) (cited by Arber) observed that the sepals part and two of them reflex forming tiny rudders, while the third remains erect and acts as a sail. These tiny craft are wafted along and may slip into the harbour of the dimple in the water made by the female flower. The pollen has a tacky exine like that of entomophilous pollen and must be brushed onto the stigmas for successful pollination to take place.

The Canadian Water-weed, *Elodea canadensis* also exhibits surface hydrophily, but differs in that its pollen is shed onto the surface of the water. The exine is spiny and air bubbles imprisoned between the spines enable it to float and keep it dry, thereby increasing its chance of reaching its destination.

A rare native plant, *Najas marina* and the introduced *N. graminea* are both truly hydrophilous and are annuals, which is rather unusual among aquatics. The female flower is a naked ovary with two to four elongated stigmas but the male retains two features of the surface chasmogams, a tiny two-lipped perianth and a spathe about its single stamen. There is only one ovule in the carpel, and Jaeger (1961) notes that hydrophilous plants often show a similar disproportion in pollen and ovule production as do the anemophilous plants. Hutchinson regards these particular species as very advanced aquatics. Arber (1920) cites Bailey as having seen pollen of *Najas graminea* whirled about in a manner which would aid pollination, by the movements of a colony of Vorticellidae which was attached to the plant, and she comments that the development of underwater relationships of this kind may prove just as important for survival as that between insects and flowers on land. This might prove a fascinating line of inquiry.

RAIN POLLINATION

The significance of rain as a pollinating agent has only recently been recognized. Hagerup (1950) finds that in the Faroes, Creeping Buttercup (*Ranunculus repens*) and Bog Asphodel (*Narthecium ossifragum*) flowers may be seen wide open on even rainy days. In this region the rain falls mostly as very gentle and frequent showers and this is of great importance in the pollination of these flowers. *R. repens* in Britain is a typical entomophilous flower with the usual positive attributes of bright colour and scent, ample provision of pollen and a little nectar too. The dehiscence of the anthers is extrorse, so in the ordinary way it cannot touch the stigmas of the central dome of carpels. The greater part of the petal is glossy and non-absorbent to water, but at the base there is a dull area with a nectary hidden under a small flap. If a raindrop falls on the flower, it dislodges pollen from the anthers on the glossy part of the petal and runs down it and is then held by the matt absorbent base. Each additional drop swirls the floating pollen around the corolla cup which may become filled with water to the level of the glossy parts. The disposition of the carpels is such that the water rises by capillarity between them and the pollen is deposited on the stigma. There is a leak of water through the gaps between the bases of the imbricated petals so that just so much water is held in the cup as is necessary for pollination.

The mechanism is slightly different in *N. ossifragum*. Here the abundant hairs on the filaments of the stamens hold the water drops. The drop bridges the gap between the dehisced anther and the central stigma and the pollen floats over on the meniscus. Both these mechanisms are successful, for the flowers set abundant seed in this area where pollinating insects are virtually absent.

CHAPTER IV

ANIMAL FOOD IN FLOWERS — POLLEN

THE COMPOSITION OF POLLEN

Pollens vary considerably in composition and probably also in food value. The data given below are those of Todd and Bretherick (1942). The chief constituents of pollen are protein, fat, carbohydrates and various inorganic mineral substances. Mustard and Dandelion pollen, both well worked by the honeybee during the peak of brood rearing in the spring are, oddly enough, not the richest in protein, but far exceed other spring pollens such as *Salix*, *Prunus communis* and *Quercus* in their fat content. This is indicated by their ether extracts of 13·13 per cent and 14·44 per cent respectively, as against 4·15, 3·15 and 6·56 per cent in the three latter genera. These percentages were obtained by the analysis of bee-collected pollen pellets in which the amounts of carbohydrates are from 20 to 48 per cent. Most of this latter is present as invert sugar and, in many cases, is not so much a pollen constituent, but is the honey regurgitated by the bees to facilitate the binding of the pollen into a pellet. This is particularly the case when bees are collecting dry, anemophilous pollen, such as that of Pine and Maize. Hand-collected pollen of *Pinus radiata* and *P. sabiniana* contain only 13 per cent (approx.) of carbohydrates, while *P. contorta* bee collected pollen contains 48·35 per cent. But Maize and Cattail (*Typha latifolia*) are genuinely rich in carbohydrates, 36·59 and 31·93 per cent respectively. Todd and Bretherick found that there was no great difference in the protein content of anemophilous and entomophilous pollen among the thirty-three species they investigated. The pollen richest in protein is that of the Date Palm, *Phoenix dactylifera*, with no less than 35·5 per cent. High protein content is also a feature of *Ceanothus crassifolius*, 29·8 per cent; of Almond, *Prunus communis*, 28·6 per cent, and Peach, *Prunus persica*, 26·48 per cent. All are very low in fat, 1–3 per cent only.

The ash fraction of pollen varies from 0·91 to 6·36 per cent with a mean of 2·7 per cent. It is richest in potassium, 20·7 per cent; then follow phosphorus, 13·6 per cent; calcium 10·5 per cent and magnesium 6·7 per cent, and lastly iron 0·07 per cent. These findings confirm those of other workers.

THE VALUE OF POLLEN AS A FOOD

Pollen is one of the two staple foods of anthophilous insects. It is their major source of protein for nectar contains but little. *Calluna vulgaris* (Ling) nectar is exceptional in having up to 1·5 per cent protein in the honey manufactured from it. Pollen is eaten by adult insects, particularly by hover flies who will perch on a petal of, say, *Nicotiana affinis*, and systematically empty one anther after another. It is also the larval food of all the bees, social or solitary, the latter provisioning a single cell with a pollen pellet on top of which the egg is laid, often floating in a film of honey. The bumble-bees (*Bombus*) either place the pollen in cells attached to clusters of the developing grubs, or store it in wax cups constructed for the purpose. Their male and queen larvae are fed frequently and individually with regurgitated nectar and pollen. This direct injection method is employed by the honey-bee to feed all larval castes. The honey-bee (*Apis*) also stores large amounts of pollen in the combs.

Many solitary bees collect pollen from a particular genus of plants or even from a single plant species: This may be a deliberate choice, for S. Taber (International Bee Keeping Congress, 1963) has extracted an "attractant" from certain pollens which hive bees seek out even when it is added to flour.

Maurizio, 1951, has shown that certain pollens are of particular biological value to the honey-bee, in that they stimulate the development of brood food glands, ovaries and the fat body, and also prolong the length of life. These include *Crocus albiflorus*,

Papaver spp., *Plantago* spp., *Pyrus* and *Trifolium* spp. and *Zea mais*. *Ranunculus* pollen, however, substantially reduced the length of life of caged bees, and indeed that of *R. puberulus* is definitely poisonous. The orange-red pollen of *Aesculus hippocastanum* has been reported as poisonous too. It would be valuable to have analyses of these pollens.

PRESENTATION OF POLLEN

The opening of the anther does not necessarily result in the presentation of pollen; an external agency may be needed, as the wind, to shake the sac in some anemophilous flowers. The active dissemination of pollen by the anther is very rare, an exception being *Ricinus* where there is differential thickening of the exothecial cells. Those near the future line of dehiscence have spiral and annular thickening which tends to resist the opening movement. On rupture of the sac, this tension is released and the anther wall recoils, violently ejecting the pollen.

(i) BY CONTRACTION OF THE ANTHER

Pollen is said to be squeezed out of the two terminal pores of *Rhododendron* anthers by contraction of the sac. The author's own observations on *Rhododendron ponticum* did not bear this out; no shrinkage was measurable 2 days after the pores opened. The pollen depends for its removal on an insect's leg or head touching the small amount exposed at the tip of the pore. On contact, the viscin threads among the tetrads stick to the insect and a long string of pollen is withdrawn from the sac. At 5 o'clock on a May morning *Bombus* queens may be seen thickly shrouded with pollen strings as they work the flowers for nectar.

(ii) BY TENSION IN THE FILAMENT

The male flower of Pellitory-of-the-wall (*Parietaria diffusa*) has four stamens the anthers of which are caught up in the four boat-shaped sepals. These latter reflex, arching the filament backwards so that it is under considerable tension. Any slight shock causes the filament to spring erect and the pollen is discharged in a "puff"—hence the name of "Artillery Plant" for this and other related species.

(iii) BY GROWTH OF STYLE

In the Compositae and Campanulaceae the anthers of the five epipetalous stamens cohere into a "box" and shed their pollen introrsely. The single style of the inferior ovary grows up through the anther box pushing the pollen out in front of it and so presenting it as a column on top of the box. The styles may be furnished with thickenings or brushes of hairs which aid in removing the pollen. Before the growth of the style, pollen may be presented by the contraction of the sensitive filaments—at least in the Compositae (*see* Biology of Androecium). The androecium of the Campanulas is not so highly organized; the filaments are not sensitive, and the anthers cohere but loosely and fall apart about one day after anther dehiscence.

(iv) BY GRADUAL AND PROGRESSIVE GAPING AND SHRINKING OF THE ANTHER WALL

Crucifers and *Epilobium hirsutum* exhibit a longitudinal split and gradual folding back of the lobes, coupled with a backward curving of the anther until a broad ribbon of pollen is available for exploitation. In Elder, (*Sambucus nigra*), *Phacelia tanacetifolia* and *Heracleum sphondylium* (Cow Parsnip), the split is followed by the complete eversion of the lobes so that a ball of pollen is produced. The Bluebell, *Endymion non-scriptus*, anther dehisces from tip to base, taking 2–4 hr to do so. *Fritillaria meleagris* is just the opposite, always dehiscing from base to tip, and again presentation is slow. The anther of *Leucojum aestivum* gapes at the tip to form a pore: later it slits longitudinally. The progressive gaping of the tops of the fused anthers of *Impatiens glandulifera* may take days to disclose all the pollen. In the barberries, the anther has a pair of ear-like flaps which are raised; the pollen comes up with the flap, leaving the shallow loculus almost empty (Fig. 19). The anther of *Limnanthes douglasii* dehisces extrorsely by a longitudinal slit, and the pollen is presented as a tacky "worm" as if pinched out of the lobe, as seeds from a violet capsule. *Bartonia aurea* shows yet another method; the oblong anther twists into a tight spiral, squeezing the pollen from the lobes.

THE ECOLOGY OF ANTHER DEHISCENCE

Anthers will dehisce over a considerable range of temperature and humidity, but both these factors may become limiting. No anther of a land plant has been seen to dehisce if it is actually *wet*. The filament may be bathed in water for half its length, as often happens in the open corollas of *Allium ursinum* after a spring shower, without affecting dehiscence.

RELATIVE HUMIDITY

Dehiscence is usually said to occur on "desiccation" of the anther tissues. In twenty-one species, including *Helleborus orientalis, Eschscholzia californica, Hypericum perforatum, Tropaeolum majus, Pyrus malus, Ribes nigrum* and *Plantago lanceolata* an r.h. of 100 per cent did not prove to be limiting for dehiscence. Another forty-three species presented pollen between 90 and 99 per cent r.h., so air, virtually saturated with water vapour, will not entirely prevent dehiscence so long as no actual precipitation occurs. The corolla of *Impatiens glandulifera, Digitalis purpurea* and the narrow-tubed varieties of *Crocosmia pottsii* afford complete protection to the anthers and dehiscence proceeds normally during rain if the temperature remains fairly high. Anther dehiscence in *Ranunculus parviflorus* is said to be brought about by the nectaries on the petals acting as osmotic hydathodes and withdrawing water from the anther by way of the filament, causing dehiscence even in very damp air. In at least two of the species mentioned above, *H. perforatum* and *P. lanceolata*, this cannot be the mechanism as the flowers are nectarless. In the aquatic, *Zannichellia*, absorption of water by the anther wall brings about dehiscence.

Structural modification of the anther wall occurs in some of the cleistogamic flowers of *Viola mirabilis* and *Oxalis acetosella*. The endothecium is reduced and does not function; the pollen grains germinate *in situ* and the tubes grow out through the anther wall. In others, the anthers are not modified and, even though the flower is cleistogamous, open normally. In the cleistogamic *Cardamine chenopodifolia* the anther wall next to the stigma degenerates and is resorbed. The anthers dehisce

71

normally in the bud stage of such self-pollinated plants as peas and beans, oats, barley and wheat. The ecology of anther dehiscence of these types is unexplored.

Observations were made on eighty-six temperate region species from January to September. A steady rise in the number of stamens ripening and presenting pollen occurred with increasing temperature; it was seldom that the limiting temperature for dehiscence could be ascertained. In *Helleborus orientalis* the lower limit is less than 1°C, while dehiscence in *Ranunculus ficaria* and *Pyrus malus* ceases at 5°C. A difficulty in assessing the limiting temperatures in the field arises from the fact that light intensity cannot be controlled. *Scilla sibirica, Leucojum aestivum, Galanthus nivalis* and *Crocus aureus* will open and present pollen at air temperatures of 4·7, 5·0, 5·0 and 4·0°C respectively if it is sunny; whereas temperatures of 8·5, 7·0, 9·4 and 9·0°C are necessary if it is dull. *Tussilago farfara, Taraxacum officinale, Plantago lanceolata* and *Ranunculus repens* all require 10°C for anther dehiscence without sun. The highest lower limit recorded was 15·3°C for partial presentation of pollen in *Epilobium adenocaulon*. No upper limits were met with.

Maturity of the anther tissues is a prerequisite for dehiscence. If an anther is fully "ripe" it will dehisce even if the surrounding air is virtually saturated with moisture. If it is not fully mature, hot sun, dry air or wind will not bring about dehiscence.

THE RHYTHM OF POLLEN PRESENTATION

Diurnal chasmogamic flowers of the north temperate regions produce their pollen chiefly from 7 a.m. to 5 p.m. but the peak period of presentation differs widely. This was established by observing some eighty-six British and exotic species over a period of years in South Wales.

DAILY LENGTH OF TIME OF POLLEN PRESENTATION

In *Helleborus orientalis* stamens dehisce any hour of the day or night and it is probable that those of the Horse Chestnut, Pear, Cherry Laurel and Fuchsia do likewise in fair weather. At the other end of the range we have *Alisma plantago-aquatica* with a presentation period of at most 4 hr and, on any one day, it may be as little as 30 min. Individual inflorescences of *Sonchus oleraceus* and *Taraxacum officinale* may present all their day's quota of pollen within 10 min.

We may divide the species according to the time and rhythm of their pollen presentation into seven groups: the "early morning", "chiefly morning", "midday", "all day", "chiefly afternoon", "afternoon" and "night" (Table 2).

The rhythm of daily presentation is a normal curve in most species with the exception of the "early morning" group where there is a great burst of anther dehiscence coincident with flower opening, then a rapid tailing off. *Senecio Jacobea* and *Centaurea nigra* may show a double peak which is a result of two batches of florets opening; in the former case they occur at 10 a.m. and noon.

Early morning group. These are species producing the bulk of their pollen before 9 a.m. and include *Calystegia sylvestris*, *Papaver dubium*, *Sarothamnus scoparius*, *Rosa spinosissima*, *Helianthemum chamaecistus*, *Clematis vitalba* and *Plantago lanceolata*.

Within the group, marked differences occur in the time of the peak period of presentation. *Calystegia* and Poppy have their maxima at 6 a.m., Broom at 7 a.m., the Rose and Rockrose at 8 a.m., Clematis between 8 and 9 a.m. and the Ribwort Plantain between 7 and 10 a.m.

Chiefly morning group. This is a big group of species including three buttercups, several Crucifers and Epilobiums, two anemones, the Welsh Gorse (*Ulex gallii*), the Dandelion and the Maize. All these plants produce from 60 to 90 per cent of their pollen by noon, and again, the peak periods vary. The three buttercups may be compared: *Ranunculus bulbosus* shows its peak (49 per cent of total production) from 9 to 10 a.m., *R. repens* (54 per cent) from 10 to 11 a.m. and *R. ficaria* (54 per cent) from 11 to 12 noon. On the other hand, those of *Anemone apennina* and *A. nemorosa* coincide at between 11 and 12 noon and at precisely 57 per cent of the total production for the day.

Midday group. This is small, comprising to date only three species: *Alisma plantago-aquatica* which produces 92 per cent of

TABLE 2—Rhyth

Species	% Presentation of pollen throughout the					
Early morning crops	4 a.m.	5 a.m.	6 a.m.	7 a.m.	8 a.m.	9 a
Calystegia sylvestris		7·2	84·5	8·1		
Papaver dubium		0·4	78·1	6·9	13·0	
Sarothamnus scoparius				39·0	8·7	
Sinapis arvensis					82·5	
Rosa spinosissima					73·4	1
Helianthemum chamaecistus		11·7	8·9	9·2	50·2	
Clematis vitalba			2·3	0·25	39·1	21
Plantago lanceolata	0·9	9·8	9·3	13·0	16·1	19
Chiefly morning crops						
Ranunculus bulbosus					12·5	28
Ranunculus repens					0·05	9
Taraxacum officinale						0
Anemone apennina						4
Anemone nemorosa						
Ranunculus ficaria						2
Aubrieta deltoides						34
Ulex gallii				1·5	18·6	19
Mid-day crops						
Alisma plantago-aquatica						
Crocus aureus						
All day crops						
Cheiranthus cheiri				2·8	2·5	6·
Rubus fruticosus					7·7	4·
Tropaeolum majus			3·1	0·4	19·6	5·
Digitalis purpurea					13·2	6·
Phacelia tanacetifolia			1·0	3·2	8·6	10·
Chiefly afternoon crops						
Pyrus malus					4·5	8·
Pyrus communis				6·4	1·1	2·
Afternoon crop						
Vicia faba						

en presentation

(peak periods shown bold)

...m.	11 a.m.	Noon	1 p.m.	2 p.m.	3 p.m.	4 p.m.	5 p.m.	6 p.m.	7 p.m.
·4									
·3	5·2	5·8	5·8	4·4	4·1	5·0	2·8		
·4	0·1	0·7					1·6		
·5	0·6		3·0						
2·3	0·3	5·9	5·3						
5·0	6·6	3·4	4·9	2·0	1·7	1·3	3·6		
2·4	5·3	4·7	3·3	2·7	1·0	0·5	1·1		
1·1	14·1	11·1	6·9	3·4	1·4	0·6	0·08		
0·0	**24·0**	12·0	11·0	5·0	5·6	1·4	0·5		
4·4	**38·5**	16·4	15·9	4·2	1·2				
6·9	**30·3**	**26·5**	10·2	7·3	3·4	0·7			
2·5	**31·3**	**26·0**	13·6	16·9	8·8	0·8			
7·1	**23·6**	**28·8**	12·6	14·0	1·3				
5·5	13·0	8·7	9·3	7·5	4·9		4·0	1·8	
3·6	9·6	10·3	8·5	4·2	5·5		5·6	3·3	
6·1	**61·7**	29·6	2·4						
	11·9	**23·4**	**22·8**	**22·4**	15·2	4·3			
6·2	9·8	17·9	18·9	16·2	10·2	6·1	2·2		
8·7	11·1	12·5	15·2	15·2	10·1	9·1	5·3	0·5	
7·7	9·3	7·2	10·0	10·6	9·9	8·2	8·9	0·8	0·1
17·0	7·8	8·0	5·3	12·8	11·8	12·2	4·7		
8·9	7·7	10·0	11·0	12·4	10·7	8·9	3·4	3·6	
7·9	7·4	12·6	13·1	17·3	12·9	11·0	4·9		
3·8	9·0	15·9	15·7	14·0	13·2	11·5	5·2	1·8	
0·4	0·8	**24·4**	**25·1**	**24·7**	16·6	5·7	2·0		

its total crop of pollen between 11 a.m. and noon, and *Arctium vulgare* and *Crocus aureus* which produce 89 and 78 per cent respectively of their pollen between noon and 2 p.m.

All day group. This is so called because pollen production is almost evenly divided between the forenoon and afternoon. Raspberry (*Rubus idaeus*), Blackberry (*R. fruticosus*) and the Loganberry (*R. loganobaccus*), the Hawthorn (*Crataegus monogyna*), Cherry Laurel (*Prunus laurocerasus*), Wallflower (*Cheiranthus cheiri*), Garden Nasturtium (*Tropaeolum majus*), Mignonette (*Reseda odorata*) and Foxglove (*Digitalis purpurea*) are all included here and their graphs of presentation show no marked peaks (Table 2).

Chiefly afternoon group. Plants presenting but 33–40 per cent of their pollen up to midday may be placed here and these include three fruit crops, Peach (*Prunus persica*), Apple (*Pyrus malus*) and Pear (*Pyrus communis*).

Afternoon group. Only two species observed so far can be classed as afternoon crops. These are *Magnolia* × *Soulangeana* and *Vicia faba* which present 84·9 per cent and 75 per cent respectively of their pollen after noon.

Night group. A "night" crop of pollen is produced by the male flowers of *Cucurbita pepo*—the Vegetable Marrow—between 10 p.m. and 3 a.m. This is the only species for which there are specific data, but many other examples of night presentation occur in the bat-pollinated flowers, including the Bignoniaceous species *Kigelia pinnata*, the Sausage Tree, and *Oroxylum indicum* (McCann, 1931), and *Adansonia digitata*, the Baobab.

THE SIGNIFICANCE OF THE POLLEN PRESENTATION RHYTHMS

We must now ascertain whether these rhythms have any significance in the animal–flower relationship. We know that honey-bees have a time sense (see Chapter VIII). Is it employed in pollen collection? Data are available. Observations both at the crop and at the hive mouth have established the curves for pollen collection. These are compared with those of pollen presentation for sixty species. Positive correlation is found in ten species, and correlation which is upset for a short period only in fifteen. In eighteen species the two curves are very similar but the peak periods do not coincide and in the remaining seventeen species there was no correlation. Therefore, there is a fair degree of correlation in 71 per cent of the species, the figure being 74 per cent for minor crops and 64 per cent for major crops. It would appear from this that the rhythm of pollen collection is reasonably well related to that of pollen presentation in individual species. Why is this so? The answer is very probably the texture of the pollen. When it is freshly presented it is in an ideal state of slight "tackiness" for rapid and complete removal and packing by the honey-bee. Because the pollen is tacky the load can be assembled without the necessity of it having to be moistened with regurgitated honey. This may be the reason why the honey-bee collects pollen as soon as it is available in the flowers whatever the time of day. The change in the consistency of pollen is well seen in *Sarothamnus scoparius*. It is tacky when the standard begins to erect, but on a dry, sunny morning it becomes powdery very quickly and a lot is blown away and lost when the flower is tripped. The collection of *Plantago lanceolata* pollen, which is a dry-skinned anemophilous type, is only possible from very freshly dehisced anthers, and even then is well moistened before it is packed by the bee.

The Duration of anther dehiscence in single flowers or flower forms ranges from 26 days in *Helleborus orientalis* to a simultaneous dehiscence of all the anthers as in *Alisma plantago aquatica*, *Papaver dubium*, *Bartonia aurea*, *Brassica oleracea*, *Rosa spinosissima*, *Aucuba japonica* and many others. The legumes also fall into this second group as total dehiscence usually occurs in the bud before the flower opens as in *Ulex europaeus*, *U. gallii* and *Sarothamnus scoparius*. They are followed by several well-known crucifers: *Sinapis arvensis*, *Raphanus raphanistrum*, *Arabis albida* and *Cheiranthus Allionii* where the period is also very short, 1–2 hr. One may note that these flowers produce all their pollen within a single foraging period, so their potential for cross pollination is very limited in time. Longer periods of anther dehiscence are, 1–2 days in *Prunus cerasus* and *Hypericum perforatum*, 1–3 in Strawberry (*Fragaria x ananassa*), *Scilla hispanica* and Foxglove (*Digitalis purpurea*), 1–4 in Blackberry and 2–5 in *Magnolia stellata*. The buttercups and anemones have long periods of anther dehiscence per flower of 2–9 days for the former and 7–14 for the latter. The capitula of the composites usually produce a fresh circlet of florets daily and overall last several days as in *Senecio Jacobaea*, 4–7 days, *Centaurea montana*, 4–10 days, and *Helianthus annuus*, 6–13 days. In contrast to this the inflorescence of Chickory (*Cichorium intybus*) lasts but 1 day. It would seem that these flowers with a longer duration of anther dehiscence are more likely to secure adequate cross-pollination.

The amount of pollen produced by a flower or "flower form" such as an inflorescence of a composite, either daily or *in toto*, varies enormously from as much as 54·7 mg in *Cucurbito pepo* to 0·005 mg in *Sonchus oleraceus*. It was not known whether the amount of pollen produced was a significant factor in its collection by bees. Observations on the honey-bee show clearly, that the amount of pollen per flower form, is of very little consequence as an "attractive" feature, compared with the presence or absence of *available nectar* in the flower. Species producing very small amounts of pollen per flower such as *Alisma plantago-aquatica* (0·06 mg), are assiduously worked for their nectar and pollen, while some of those producing abundant pollen only, such as *Eschscholzia californica* (12·9 mg total and 3·2 mg per flower per day), or whose nectar is not available, may be entirely neglected. However, in times of pollen shortage, even those flowers without nectar will be visited. These periods, for the hive-bee, occur in early spring, sometimes during the so-called "June Gap", that is between the finish of the fruit blossom and the beginning of the clover blooming, or again perhaps, in early autumn.

THE SIGNIFICANCE OF POLLEN COLLECTION FOR POLLINATION

Among the hermaphrodite and monoecious species so far investigated numbering some eighty-six in all, pollination is effected when the *honey-bee* is collecting pollen. This was so even where the dimensions of the flower and the disposition of its parts seem to render it unlikely, as in *Helleborus orientalis*, *Rhododendron ponticum* and *Magnolia × Soulangeana*. The bee

works the anthers of the last species while holding on to neighbouring ones. The spread of the stamens is too great for it to
work them from the carpel column as in *Magnolia stellata*, but
the column may be scaled in leaving the flower and pollen left
on the stigmas. The worker-bee need not touch the stigmas of
the large protogynous primary flowers of *Helleborus orientalis*
(Lenten Lily) when gathering pollen, but some were seen to
visit young flowers in which anther dehiscence had not yet
begun and work the nectaries and then return to the older
flowers. These later flowers are smaller and the bee is more
likely to come in contact with the stigmas. This behaviour is
interesting, for it is only in these later flowers of the third and
fourth order of the cyme, that a reasonable number of the
nectaries are exploitable (see Chapter V). Hive-bees, working
Rhododendron ponticum for pollen, do not always distinguish the
anthers from the stigma. One worker arrived at 9.37 a.m., left
with a good load of pollen at 9.51 a.m. and during the visit, made
four attempts to reach the nectar, scrabbled six stigmas for
pollen, and touched eight stigmas without scrabbling. So
pollination of this large bumble-bee flower is frequently effected
by its smaller relative.

CHAPTER V

ANIMAL FOOD IN FLOWERS—NECTAR AND NECTARIES

NECTAR, which in classical mythology always meant the "drink of the gods", is, in the plant world, a sugary secretion from a "nectary" and one of the two chief foods of the anthophilous animals be they insect, bird or mammal. It is not to be confused with honey which the bees manufacture from it.

THE NATURE OF NECTARIES

Recent work by Frey-Wyssling, Shuel and Zimmermann indicates that nectaries are real glands with an active metabolism and are not merely passive valves by which surplus sap is excreted by the plant. For example, Shuel (1956) kept the cut stalks of Snapdragon buds in different sugars for 4 days, that is, until they were fully open. This is the period during which the nectar is secreted. When the buds were supplied with sucrose only, both fructose and glucose were present, although not plentiful, in the secreted nectar. When fructose and glucose were supplied, large amounts of sucrose were present in the nectar. Zimmermann (1953) obtained similar results with *Impatiens holstii*, only pure sucrose being secreted when the flowering shoots were standing in glucose or fructose solutions, although entirely "foreign" sugars, such as arabinose, were absorbed and excreted unchanged by the nectaries. Both results suggest that sugars have been transformed in the nectaries. Final confirmation comes from Frey-Wyssling, Zimmermann and Maurizio (1954) who used excised nectaries of *Euphorbia pulcherrima* which they floated on a 5 per cent solution of C^{14} glucose. The nectar was sampled at intervals and analysed chromatographically to separate the component sugars which were then scanned for radioactivity. The C^{14} molecule appeared in all the three sugars, sucrose, fructose and glucose. This is unexceptional evidence of a rebuilding of sugars within the nectary by enzyme action. A transfructosidase is present in the secreted nectar.

Nectaries are very varied in siting and form. Many are situated outside the flower, as are those in the angle between the midrib and main veins, on the back of the cherry laurel, *Prunus laurocerasus*, leaf. Passion flowers have curious stalk-like nectaries on their petioles, while in the vetches they are in the form of small depressions on the back of the stipules. All these are **extra-floral nectaries**. They may play an important role in the insect–plant relationship, which is not always to the advantage of the plant (see under Nectar Concentration).

The Partridge Pea, *Cassia chamaecrista*, has a saucer-shaped nectary on the upper surface of the petiole which may secrete for 3 months and which in the dry regions of Georgia is the main source of nectar for bees. The flower is nectarless!

Nectaries are not the sole perquisite of the flowering plant. The bracken, *Pteridium aquilinum*, has a smooth, shining nectary at the point where each pinna joins the rachis. This secretes abundant nectar, and is an important source of food for the honey-bee in some upland parts of Wales where no other spring forage is available.

One might even consider the Ergot Fungus *Claviceps purpurea* to be "nectariferous", as it too, secretes a sweet fluid in the early stages of its development, as do the pycnidia of the Rust Fungus *Puccinia poarum*.

FLORAL NECTARIES

Any organ of the flower may be modified into a nectary or bear nectariferous tissue.

SEPAL NECTARIES

In *Paeonia*, the sepals are not modified in any way from the normal leaf-like form, but, nevertheless, secrete nectar which ants exploit even before the flower, which is nectarless, opens. An extreme condition occurs in *Thunbergia grandiflora* where the calyx is just a ring of nectar-secreting tissue. If ants are

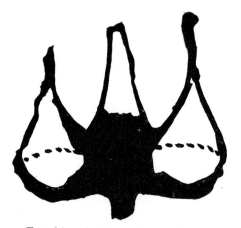

FIG. 34. *Abutilon striatum*. L.S. of calyx cup. × 2. The nectary lines the base up to the dotted line.

present on the calyx, as they usually are, they deter the *Xylocopa* bees from robbing the flower by piercing the base of the corolla tube (Pijl, 1954).

Sepal nectaries are a feature of several genera of the Malvaceae; these include *Abutilon*, *Pavonia* and *Lavatera*. In *Abutilon megapotamicum* the gamosepalous calyx has a basal five-pointed star of nectar tissue, the points of the star being opposite the very narrow slits between the claws of the petals. The right-angled bend in the calyx of *A. striatum* forms a cup which fits tightly against the petals, and prevents access to the nectar except by means of a narrow slit between the petal bases. The bottom of the cup is lined to a depth of 3 mm by the nectary; the cup itself is about 8 mm in depth (Fig. 34). Each sepal of

Lavatera olbia has a discrete patch of secreting tissue. Dense hairs fringe the petal base and possibly prevent the access of tiny insects. Despite the hairs, a large bead of nectar often wells out from between the petals.

PETAL NECTARIES

These occur throughout the Ranales and the nearly allied Berberidales. In *Ranunculus* itself the nectary is situated under a tiny flap of tissue near the base of the petal; this is the simplest type. The *Aquilegia* petal is coloured and retains its petaloid form at the top, but the base is prolonged into a narrow curved tube which terminates in a solid knob of secreting tissue. *Helleborus* has a petal which is not colourful but herbaceous, and tubular above a short-stalked base (Fig. 8). It fills from a half to two-thirds of its length with concentrated nectar (26–41 per cent) of pure sucrose. The lips of the tube of 84 per cent of the petals of primary flowers of *Helleborus orientalis* are pinched together so tightly that they cannot be exploited. Honey-bees, gathering pollen on the primaries in February, went frequently to the smaller flowers of the third and fourth order on the cyme, where only 35 per cent of the tubes were occluded, to obtain nectar with which to bind the pollen together.

STAMINAL NECTARIES

The Violas have staminal nectaries in the form of two slender tongues of green tissue arising on the filaments of two of the stamens. These project backwards into the spurred petal which receives their secretion. The spur tissue does not secrete. In *Anemone pulsatilla* the anthers of a few of the outermost stamens secrete nectar instead of producing pollen, but *A. nemorosa* is nectarless.

CARPEL NECTARIES

There are three distinct types of carpel nectary descriptively named "valve", "septal" and "disc". The "valve" nectary of *Caltha palustris* is simply a groove of secreting tissue on the flanks and towards the base of the young carpel.

The "septal" nectary is associated chiefly with the tricarpellary ovary of the Liliales and their derivatives. The young ovary has three vertical grooves marking the position of the septa.

Nectar is secreted along these lines and appears as beads of liquid which run down the groove and collect around the base of the ovary in the cup of the perianth. In *Endymion non-scriptus*, where the perianth parts only overlap, the honey-bee soon learns to slip its tongue in between their bases and so steal the nectar.

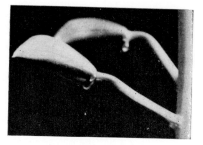

Fig. 35. *Cymbidium* sp., Orchidaceae. Nectar drops excreted below tepals and at the base of ovary prior to flowering. ×0·4.

In some irises and orchids, which have inferior ovaries, large beads of nectar may be seen on the outside of the flower (Fig. 35), but the top of the ovary also secretes and lessens this apparent disadvantage.

Veltheimia viridifolia is unusual in that nectar may be secreted *inside* as well as outside the ovary. If the top of the ovary is cut off after anther dehiscence is complete but before the stigma is receptive, beads of liquid may be seen on the midribs of the *valves* of the carpels. There was abundant nectar in the loculi of the ovary of a flower which had only one or two ovules per carpel, instead of the usual four or five. On chromatographic analyses, it proved to be of the same type as the external secretion, chiefly fructose and glucose with a little sucrose. In another flower, in which the ovules were not counted, the concentration of the nectar, within and without the ovary, was the same, namely 15 per cent.

A somewhat different carpellary nectary is that of the Umbellifers. Here, the inferior ovary is surmounted by a thick pad, or "disc" of secreting tissue through which the styles peep. The secretion of the disc of *Hedera helix* often crystallizes and can be removed as a sugary cast of the nectary.

RECEPTACLE NECTARIES
The receptacular cups of the perigynous Rosaceae and Saxifragaceae are usually lined with nectar tissue which secretes abundantly in many of the former (Raspberry, Blackberry, Plum), but scantily in the latter.

AXIAL NECTARIES
The bicarpellate gamopetalous orders, namely the Lamiales, Personales and Solanales, have the nectary in the form of a circlet of secreting tissue embracing, and more or less fused to, the base of the ovary.

Sesamum alatum is unusual in that sterile flowers are clustered at the base of the leaf petioles and their only function appears to be the secretion of nectar (Hagerup, 1932).

THE COMPOSITION OF NECTAR

Nectar chiefly contains sugar, with, in specific cases, small amounts of organic acids, ethereal oils, polysaccharides such as dextrin, protein and enzymes, boron (in *Nymphaea*), and alkaloids.

The predominant sugars are sucrose and its breakdown products, fructose and glucose. Very much smaller quantities of raffinose, maltose, melibiose, trehalose (in *Carex*) and melezitose may also be present. Raffinose is found commonly in the Ranales and their derivatives, the barberries and fumitories. Indeed, a sucrose nectar, with the single oligosaccharide raffinose, could almost be safely said to be Ranalian. Melibiose is quite common in Boraginaceae and in the genus *Lonicera*, and has been found in all nectars of the Dipsacaceae so far examined.

The proportions of the major sugars vary greatly, ranging from the virtually pure sucrose nectar of the hellebores to the nectar of the Cruciferae which only contains glucose and fructose. The nectar of long-tubed flowers is chiefly sucrose together with smaller amounts of glucose and fructose. It is these flowers, with deep-seated, protected nectar, which are especially associated with the highest classes of insects, the bumble- and honey-bees, butterflies and moths. In contrast to this, shallow flowers with relatively unprotected nectar usually have a preponderance of the two monosaccharides and but little sucrose.

The type of nectar is sometimes a feature of the plant family as a whole, and families which are closely related often have the same kind of nectar. For example, the Ranunculaceae, Helleboraceae, Berberidaceae and Fumariaceae, which Hutchinson places together at the bottom of his "Herbaceae" have almost pure sucrose nectar. On the other hand, the climax groups of the Cruciferae, Umbelliferae, a section of the Compositae (Asterae), the Euphorbiales and the herbaceous Rosaceae have a simple sugar nectar of equal parts of fructose and glucose. One may note that the family characteristic overrules that of the flower type, for even long deep flowers among the Cruciferae (e.g. *Lunaria biennis*) have the monosaccharide nectar, and "open" flowers, such as buttercups, have the sucrose nectar as well as the hellebores with their long-tubed petal nectaries.

It is particularly interesting to see that these highly evolved families are producing a nectar which is *technically* a honey, and which needs no action by the digestive enzymes of the anthophilous insect to convert it into "available" food. It would be interesting to know whether this has any significance for the insects.

At the species level Wykes (1952b) and Percival (1962) find that the type of nectar secreted is remarkably constant. Only 61 species out of 889 tested were found to have nectar varying in composition. This is true even when the plants are growing in different localities in the British Isles. It may not hold on a continental scale.

Among the plants with variable nectar, the Salices (Willows) are interesting because in *Salix atrocinerea* and *S. caprea* the male catkins have a sucrose-dominated nectar, while the female catkins have fructose and glucose predominating. The female trees of three other species also have this latter type. Furgala (1958) and co-workers, using a quantitative method of determination, have found marked variation in composition within crops of legumes, which they attribute to variation in environmental conditions during the sampling period. Quoting from their figures, in *T. pratense* (Red Clover) the range is sucrose 57–88 per cent, glucose 2–27 per cent and fructose 7–23 per cent. However, the *type* of nectar remains sucrose-dominated and hence, unchanged.

Zimmermann (1953, 1954) has shown that enzymes, both transfructosidases and transglucosidases, are present in certain nectars and one may perhaps assume that the variations in nectar composition result from their activities, and that this accounts for both inter- and intra-specific variation.

COMPOSITION OF NECTAR AND AGE OF FLOWER

Two cases of a change in nectar composition with age may be mentioned. The nectar of young flowers with anther dehiscence half completed of *Hibiscus syriaca* had sucrose dominating over the monosaccharides, that of closing flowers with dehiscence completed had more fructose in it than sucrose or glucose. Rosser (1952) found a change in *Fuchsia hybrida Hort.* nectar, the fructose–glucose ratio rising from 2·183 on the first day of the flower's life, to 4·041 on the fourth. One may contrast this with the constancy of the nectar of *Helleborus orientalis*. The tubed petal nectaries remain fresh on the flower for 3 weeks. The nectar is pure sucrose and it was not until the third week that a very small amount of raffinose was detected in it.

Nectar changes which occur on ageing can have little significance for the flower visitor, as flowers will normally be exploited as soon as nectar is available in them.

SIGNIFICANCE OF THE COMPOSITION OF NECTAR IN FLORAL BIOLOGY

We now come to the question as to whether the composition of nectar has any significance in flower life. Wykes (1952a) offered honey-bees, confined in cages, various mixtures of sugars and found that consistent preferences were shown for single sugars in the following descending order: sucrose, glucose, maltose, fructose. When a mixture was offered, the bees showed an anomalous high preference for sucrose–glucose–fructose solutions, an equal mixture of these proving the most attractive. Furgala's (1958) findings seem to confirm this, for he notes that *Melilotus alba*, whose nectar has this balance of sugars, is preferred to Lucerne, Alsike and Red Clover, where sucrose is dominant.

This "SFG" mixture of sugars is found in most of the so-called "bee" flowers, but the proportions differ, being roughly S : F : G as 2:1:1. An equal mixture is quite uncommon.

An analysis of the nectar of ninety-two crops especially well worked by the honey-bee in Britain showed forty-six species were of the sucrose dominant type and forty-three species of the fructose–glucose dominant type. The remaining three crops had "variable" nectar. None had the balanced nectar, so the bees had no opportunity to exercise their choice.

CONCENTRATION OF NECTAR

The concentration of the sugars in nectar is of primary importance in the animal–flower relationship. It governs the visits of the higher insects of the honey- and bumble-bee classes. The late J. Pryce-Jones calculated that below 18 per cent of sugar in the nectar, the honey-bees "work at a loss". There is abundant evidence to show that, other things being equal, the honey-bee, *Apis mellifera*, will always exploit the crops with the more concentrated nectar. Furthermore, Von Frisch (1950) has shown that the concentration of the nectar affects the behaviour of the bees, particularly the vigour of the bee-dances which conditions the number of worker-bees recruited to forage the crop. After returning from foraging to the hive, the bees disgorge their sacs and, if the nectar gathered has a low percentage of sugar, they may not dance at all. If they return with concentrated nectar, they dance and attract the attention of their fellows. The vigour of the dance increases as the concentration.

Table 3 shows nectar concentrations found in some British and exotic species. The variation is very great, ranging from the virtually supersaturated (74 per cent) nectar of the Horse Chestnut, *Aesculus hippocastunum*, to the weak nectars of Plum (10–28 per cent) and Primrose (5–15 per cent). The figures also show that there is great variation within a single species. Solanaceae, Scrophulariaceae, Acanthaceae, Boraginaceae and Labiatae, with deep-seated nectar have, as a whole, concentrated nectars with sugar content ranging from 16–55 per cent, i.e.

TABLE 3

Concentration of nectar in British and exotic species, together with type of pollinator and amount of nectar secreted per flower

Species / British Plants	Type of pollinator	Av. amount nectar in mg/fl	Av. per cent sugar
Primula vulgaris	bee-fly		5–15
Oenothera biennis	moth		8
Prunus laurocerasus	promiscuous pollination		9–32
Prunus avium	honey- or bumble-bee		12
Chaemaenerion angustifolium	honey-bee		13
Rubus idaeus	honey-bee		12–24
Prunus domestica	honey-bee		16
Prunus domestica (culti-vated vars.)	honey-bee		10–28
Vicia sepium	bumble-bee		17–50 plus
Knautia arvensis	honey- + bumble-bee		19·5
Lythrum salicaria	bumble-bee		21·5
Trifolium pratense	bumble-bee		22·5
Prunus spinosa	honey-bee		24
Epilobium hirsutum	honey-bee		25
Lotus conrniculatus	honey-bee		25–50 plus
Dipsacus follonum ssp. *sylvestris*	bumble-bee		26
Ribes uva-crispa	honey-bee		30
Trifolium medium	bumble-bee		31·5
Trifolium repens	honey-bee		41
Malus sylvestris, various vars.	honey-and bumble-bees, *Andrenas*		50
Brassica rapa	honey-bee		50·5
Taraxacum officinale	honey-bee		51
Salix spp.	honey-bee, *Andrenas*		60

(50, 50·5, 51, 60 bracketed with note: American figs.)

Exotic species			
Aloë arborescens	bird	54·5	13
Musa velutina, hermaphro-dite flower	bat	104	14
Musa velutina male flower	bat	150	16
Jasminium polyanthum	moth	5	18
Clianthus puniceus	bird		19·5
Leonotis leonurus	bird	17·5	20
Manettia inflata	bird	18	20
Acanthus mollis	carpenter-bee	163	20
Plumbago rosea	butterfly	3	21·5
Eucharis grandiflora	moth?	22·5	21
Citrus paradisi	honey-bee	32	21·5
Abutilon megapotamicum	bird	109	22
Salvia rutilans	bird?	3	27
Billbergia nutans	bird	40	30
Citrus sinensis (Navel Orange)	honey-bee		30
Coleus thyrsoideus	bee	3	34
Euphorbia fulgens		7	35
Lachenalia aloides	bird	11	39·5
Asclepias curassavica	butterfly	11	48
Euphorbia pulcherrima			60
Robinia pseudacacia	honey-bee		63
Aesculus hippocastanum	honey-bee, bumble-bee queens		33–74

nearly always well above the lower limit for economic exploitation. As may be anticipated, these variations in nectar concentration introduce an element of competition between plants for the pollinators, not only at the species level but also at the varietal. This latter sometimes has undesirable consequences in economic crops.

Among plums, the varieties Maynard, Eldorado and Milton have nectar containing 10·1, 14·9 and 28·4 per cent of sugar respectively. In a mixed orchard of these varieties, Milton attracted most bees and was well pollinated. We may note, moreover, that it would receive pollen from its own race, as honey-bees are markedly constant to a particular source. This conservatism is of great importance in the biology of the flower, and has its attending advantages and also dangers. Taking a hypothetical case, if a variety is self-fertile, and its nectar has a high sugar content, its "pollination potential" is very high if honey-bees are the visitors. If, however, the variety is self-sterile, and has either (a) a very high or (b) a very low percentage of sugar in the nectar, its "pollination potential" will be very low. If (a) pertains the bees will crowd on to the tree and it will receive its own pollen which is ineffectual. If (b) pertains, no honey-bee visitors will come bearing effective pollen from another variety. Indeed, it would only succeed biologically, if it was competing on even terms, as regards nectar concentration, with neighbouring varieties. It is a common practice to plant a mixture of varieties of pears or apples in an orchard to ensure the presence of compatible pollen for all. Yet a marked variation in nectar concentration might set this precaution at naught. We must remember, however, that early spring, in the north temperate zone, is a time of comparative scarcity of both nectar and pollen. This offsets the potential danger of inequalities in nectar concentration in two ways. Firstly, the crop may be visited for pollen alone, and secondly, Butler (1945) has shown, if demand exceeds supply and if an orchard is flooded with bees, a wandering population is created which greatly increases the chance of cross-pollination.

COMPETITION BETWEEN FLORAL AND EXTRAFLORAL NECTARIES

Differences in nectar concentration as between floral and extrafloral nectar may be disadvantageous to the pollination of the flowers. Vansell working in Oregon gives the following example. In the common vetch the concentration of the flower nectar is 22·6 per cent sugar as against 56·5 per cent of the stipular: Hungarian vetch blossom nectar shows 25·2 per cent sugar, the stipular nectar 47·7 per cent. Bees work the stipular nectaries of both species assiduously and neglect the flowers.

QUANTITY OF NECTAR AND FACTORS AFFECTING IT

Generally speaking, small flowers secreting small amounts of nectar, are a feature of the north temperate zone. Pre-eminent among them are the clovers and the blackberries. The bulk of the large-flowered species with copious nectar occur in the subtropics and the southern hemisphere. Prominent among these are the calyciferous monocotyledons (i.e. those with sepals and petals), particularly the Banana (*Musa* spp.), whose tubular flower fills nearly to the brim. Other examples are the nearly related Crane Flower, *Strelitzia reginae*, and the Heliconias.

We may also include the *Proteas* where nectar is poured into the cup of the inflorescence bracts from flowers individually small. Famous "honey flowers" in South Africa are species of *Melianthus*—a shrubby genus with long racemes of medium-sized flowers with zygomorphic calyces. These latter fill with nectar (from the sepal nectaries) which rains down if the flowers are shaken.

It is proven that as long as sufficient nectar is available bees, at least, tend to remain "fixed" to a crop. So the quantity of nectar produced is important; and this is obviously partly dependent on the length of the flowering period.

At the species level Beutler (1953) states that the size of the nectary and the amount of nectar are positively correlated. If we compare Raspberry (*Rubus idaeus*) and Blackberry (*Rubus fruticosus*) the former has larger nectaries and yields more nectar than the latter. This is scarcely of practical significance, as they flower at different times and do not compete with one another for pollinators. But in varieties of citrus fruits where a similar relationship holds, it may be otherwise. Fahn's (1949) results show that *C. sinensis v. Valencia* with a nectary of 14 mm³ secreted 28 mg (dry weight) of nectar, and variety Shamouti with a nectary of 8 mm³, only 6 mg.

THE POSITION OF THE FLOWER ON THE PLANT

There is conflicting evidence as to whether real differences exist between the amount of nectar secreted by flowers on different parts of a plant. Beutler and Wahl (1936) found that, although the flowers from the topmost branches of a lime tree gave less nectar than those from below, the nectar was more concentrated. Andreev (1928) found that the bottom flowers of the racemose inflorescences of Phacelia have bigger nectaries and secrete more nectar than those at the tip. One would expect the opposite in cymose inflorescences for here the topmost flowers open first, and these, as in racemes, are usually the largest and longest-lived, and also have the stoutest pedicels. It has already been established that Blackberry flowers on stout shoots, yield more nectar than those on thin shoots, and this relationship very probably also applies to thick and thin pedicels.

NECTAR YIELD AND AGE OF FLOWER

Nectar secretion varies with the age of the flower. Fahn (1949) finds that the secretion is greatest in amount on the first day and least on the last day, of the flower's life in Navel and Bergamot Oranges and *Callistemon lanceolatus*. Secretion in *Acanthus mollis* (Table 4) builds up from a modest start on the first day to a high level for the next 5 days and then begins to tail off. The observations were not continued after the ninth day. On the third day the weather changed from "warm and dry" to "cool and windy", which probably accounts for the low figure. What is interesting, is that the percentage of sugar in the nectar *increases* as the flower ages, so its attraction for insects does not diminish. This is important for the pollination of this exotic species in Britain, because the style does not move downward, nor do the stigma valves open until the flower is at least a week old (Fig. 30). By this time the flower looks far from attractive as the pale-coloured lower lip of the corolla is dried out and papery, yet *Bombus agrorum* continued to visit the "dead" flowers and proved an efficient pollinator.

TABLE 4. Nectar secretion in *Acanthus mollis*

No. of flowers	Date	Total amount of nectar per day in mg	Average % of sugar
5	31/7/61	67·25	27·3*
	1/8/61	109·75	20·7
	2/8/61	72·25	23·4
	3/8/61	96·25	23·3
	4/8/61	111·00	24·5
	5/8/61	87·5	24·7
	6/8/61	63·75	26·9
	7/8/61	50·0	31·6
	8/8/61	58·0	28·2

* Four samples only, one too small for estimation

Raw (1953) found that removal of nectar from the flowers of *Rubus fruticosus* and *R. idaeus* resulted in a more copious flow of weaker nectar. Pedersen (1961) suggests that it may be possible to assess the extent to which two crops of alfalfa are being pollinated by sampling the nectar and seeing how the concentration compares the one with the other. A high concentration may indicate that the crop is being ignored by the bees.

Vansell and co-workers found that Orange blossom secretes nectar in the bud stage but, generally speaking, nectar secretion is greatest at the time of anthesis and the advantage accruing to the plant is obvious.

As the inflorescences of *Salvia leucantha* (Fahn, 1949) and *Rubus fruticosus* agg, the amount of nectar produced by successive flowers decreases.

NECTAR YIELD AND AGE OF PLANT

Wadey (1961) draws attention to the fact that Lime trees, *Tilia europaea,* in East Sussex which were famous for their nectar yield 80–100 years ago, have, in recent times, been

Fig. 36. *Musa velutina.* Bird or Bat flower type. Four pale yellow male flowers with exerted stamens subtended by a reflexed pink bract. The tubular perianth fills ·5–·75 with nectar; average 150 mg, 16 per cent sugar. ×0·63.

virtually deserted by the honey-bees which now visit neighbouring young trees 20–40 years old. This indicates that little nectar is being produced by the old trees. A similar falling-off in nectar production is evident in ageing Blackberry plantations and old wild White Clover meadows. The reason for this is unexplained.

SEX OF FLOWER AND NECTAR PRODUCTION

In several monoecious plants there are differences in the amount of nectar secreted by the male and female flowers. Fahn (1949) found that the male flowers of Banana, *Musa paradisiaca*, secreted 422 mg of liquid nectar (dry wt. 119 mg) as against 102 mg (26 mg dry wt.) secreted by the females. In three members of the Cucurbitaceae the position was reversed, the female flowers secreting on an average 163 mg of nectar, compared with 39 mg secreted by the males. This was attributed to the size of the nectaries; in Banana the male flower has the larger nectary, in the cucurbitas, the female.

But perhaps this is not the whole story, for in *Musa velutina*, where the difference between the size of the nectaries in the male and hermaphrodite flowers is in the other direction, the male flowers still secrete more and the concentration of sugars is a little higher.

Musa velutina	Diameter of nectary mm	Amount of nectar mg	% of sugar in nectar
Male flowers	3·6	150	16
Hermaphrodite flowers	4·6	104·2	14·4

INTRASPECIFIC DIFFERENCES IN NECTAR PRODUCTION

We have already mentioned varietal differences in nectar concentration in Plum, but the *amount* of sugar secreted differs in Raspberry, Apple and Cherry varieties. Beutler and Schöntag (1940), sampling not less than a hundred flowers, found that among eight varieties of Apple the daily production of nectar varied from 1·8 to 6·2 mg/sugar/flower and among three varieties of Cherry from 1·95 to 3·6 mg/sugar/flower.

This might not have any value beyond holding the pollinators *longer* to the better supplies of nectar. The concentration of the nectar is the foremost consideration.

FLOWER COLOUR AND NECTAR SECRETION

There are certain varietal differences in nectar secretion which are associated with flower colour. Stadler (1886) said that the dark pink variety of Indian Balsam, *Impatiens glandulifera*, secretes more nectar than the pale pink, and also that a red form of *Asclepias syriaca*, the Milkweed, secretes more than the white.

Among the legumes, however, Goetze (1930) found that white sports of Red and Crimson Clover and of Alfalfa are superior to the type in nectar production. This could be quite an important factor in the flower–bee relationship, as bees have a highly developed colour sense which is employed in building up the pattern conditioning its flower visits.

NECTAR SECRETION AND POLYPLOIDY

Maurizio (1954) has investigated the nectar and nectar production of diploid and polyploid strains of five species of Clover, two species of Datura, *Lobelia syphilitica* and two Salvias. She finds that although the diploids had more concentrated nectar, the amount of sugar secreted per flower per day is 1·3–4·4 times greater in the polyploids. In *Salvia splendens*, where diploid, triploid, tetraploid and octoploid races were compared, the quantity of both nectar and sugar per flower per day increased with the degree of polyploidy. The polyploid races tend to produce fewer flowers than the diploid, but their flowering period is often longer; so, taking it all in all, the polyploids are superior to the diploids as a nectar crop. The floral biological significance of these facts may be considerable, but there is still another facet. The colours of flowers of polyploid races are sometimes, *plus vif* as Vilmorin of Paris describes his *Nemesias*. This again may be significant in view of the colour sense of bees.

THE ECOLOGY OF NECTAR SECRETION

The potentiality for nectar secretion is hereditary. Whether it is fulfilled depends on the plant's environment which is composed of climatic and edaphic factors. It is well known by beekeepers that a species may secrete heavily in one part of its geographic range, and lightly, or not at all in another. *Calluna vulgaris* is a case in point; migratory beekeepers wishing to exploit it for the production of the high-priced heather honey, will not take their hives to a fringe area, but rather well into a central area of heather moors. The reasons underlying these differences in nectar secretion are unknown, and only detailed autecological studies will reveal them.

THE EFFECT OF SOLAR RADIATION ON NECTAR SECRETION

According to Shuel (1955) there is a direct immediate effect of solar radiation on nectar secretion. In clover, a sunny day is seen to boost secretion, and a dull day to depress it. He argues that as nectar sugars are products of photosynthesis, and as photosynthesis is dependent on the sun's energy, this is exactly what one would expect. Beutler, Von Czarnowski and Shuel (1957) grew Rape (*Brassica napus* v. *arvensis*) in identical nutrient water culture solutions in Munich, Berlin and Guelph (Canada). They found that the greater the energy of radiation received by the crop, the more nectar sugar was secreted unless the radiation was "too strong" (data not given) when sugar production was not encouraged. It is curious to note, however, that plants which were receiving the *same* intensity of radiation in Munich and Guelph, secreted more nectar at the latter station. Species differ in their response to insolation. In Cuba the finest nectar plant, the white "Campanula" (*Ipomoea sidaefolia*), secretes best during hot days with bright sunshine, but in another Cuban plant, the Coral Vine (*Antigonon leptopus*), strong insolation diminishes the flow as the day wears on, and flow is continuous on cloudy days.

THE EFFECT OF RELATIVE HUMIDITY

This is primarily connected with the shape of the flower. Nectar, deep-seated in tubed flowers, is largely protected from the external environment and unaffected by changes in it. In shallow flowers with unprotected nectar, changes in relative humidity, rain or air movement may affect the concentration and may radically alter the pollination potential of the flowers. A case in point comes from America. In the morning in California when the relative humidity is high, Orange blossom nectar only contains 16 per cent of sugar. The bees ignore it, preferring Cabbage, *Brassica campestris*, Radish, *Raphanus sativus*, and Horehound, *Marrubium vulgare*, with nectars of 45 per cent or more sugar. By midday in the hot sun the r.h. decreases and the exposed nectar in the Orange concentrates to 25–50 per cent.

When the concentration reaches 30 per cent the bees forsake the weeds for the Orange. (Vansell, Walters and Bishop, 1942.)

SOIL MOISTURE

In the temperate regions, the level of soil humidity is seldom a *limiting* factor to secretion, but it may be sub-optimal. Optimal levels probably vary with the species and may differ widely but data are scarce. Andrejevna cited by Veprikov (1936) shows that a soil moisture content between 45 and 75 per cent is most favourable for nectar production in red clover. Fahn (1949) finds that nectar secretion of *Antirrhinum* flowers remains steady as the wilting point approaches, but is much reduced for a whole day *after* watering. Then, on the second day, the original level is largely regained. The time lag is greater in Pomegranate and Knapweed. If watered when "dry" they take 2 days to show an increase in secretion. In Cuba Sesame responds the next day to showers. There are many reports of nectar flows failing in drought, from that of Gum trees (Eucalyptus) in Western Australia, to that of the flora of the Danube meadows in Bulgaria. The consequences of the failure of a particular source may be far more serious for the animals dependent on the crop than for the plant itself.

THE INFLUENCE OF TEMPERATURE ON NECTAR SECRETION

French, Israeli and Russian workers generally agree that a rise in air temperature increases nectar production. Many plants show a threshold value below which they will not *begin* to secrete. This is 8°C for *Prunus avium*, 18°C for *Prunus laurocerasus* (Beutler, 1953, citing Behlen). However, once secretion has started, it may be maintained even if the temperature drops very considerably, 1–5°C in the case of the Cherry Laurel. An upper threshold exists too: White Clover may not yield nectar if the summer temperature exceeds 25°C. This was proved in North America, where it is an introduced crop, by checking the honey yields north and south of the 25°C isotherm. Yields were good to the north. So a transplant may fail in a new environment if the range of temperature is so different from that of its native home that it can afford insects no reward for their visits. There is an old beekeeper's saying that "cool nights and warm days promote the flow of nectar". Certainly *Tilia*, growing under natural conditions, secretes more sugar during cool nights (Beutler, 1953).

PLANT NUTRITION AND NECTAR SECRETION

It is only recently that the effect of nutrition on nectar secretion has been explored by means of replicated experiments where the interaction of the main nutrients could be analysed statistically. Both Shuel (1956) and Ryle (1954) have shown that not only is it necessary to know the relative levels of supply of the main salts to the plant, but also, in the case of perennials, the nutrition of previous years, before it is possible to ascertain the effect of any one element on the nectar secretion. The following quotation from Shuel's (1957) summary of his work on Red Clover and *Antirrhinum* may be taken as largely representing the findings of both authors:

"For maximal production of nectar by the plant, the following conditions of fertility would appear desirable: a level of nitrogen low enough to avoid excessive vegetative growth, a level of phosphorus sufficient to promote good flowering, and a level of potassium which is neither low enough to limit growth severely nor high enough to reduce flower production."

CHAPTER VI

POLLINATION BY
BIRDS (Ornithophily)

BIRDS differ from the anthophilous insects in that they can obtain only one of their two staple foods from the flowers. This is nectar, and a Humming-bird can take up to half its weight in sugar daily. They do not take pollen except incidentally while sipping nectar. They collect some of their protein food, such as small insects, on the petals or in the tubes of the flowers; or they exploit the abundance of minute aquatic life, which flourishes in the liquid which collects within the overlapping floral bracts of the Heliconias (Strelitziaceae) (Beebe, 1950). Spiders, too, form an important fraction of their animal food. The two bumble-bee sized nestlings of *Calypte costae*, the Costa humming bird, are fed entirely upon small spiders by the henbird for the first week of their lives, and then their diet is changed to one of regurgitated nectar (Walker and Young, 1934). The birds require a terrain which will furnish them with both their carbonhydrate and protein needs; namely an abundant and continuous supply of insects and arachnids, and a succession of flowers throughout the year. There are regions in three continents where these conditions pertain; the equatorial belt in America, i.e. 5° North and South of the equator, which is the main centre of the Humming-birds (Trochilidae); the tropics and subtropics of Africa, the home of the Sun-birds (Nectarinidae); the Sugarbirds (Promeropidae) of South Africa, and the S.W. Pacific where the Honey-eaters (Meliphagidae), are concentrated. These four families comprise the bulk of the birds which appear to be most highly adapted to visiting flowers. There is also a highly evolved though smaller group of Honey-creepers (Drepanididae), in the Hawaiian Islands. The Brush-tongued Lories and Lorikeets (Loriinae) of Eastern Australia and Tasmania are important flower visitors. Other fringe groups are the "White-eyes" or "Silver-eyes" (Zosteropidae) in Africa and Australia and the Tanagers (Thraupidae) in Central and South America.

The Humming-birds (Trochilidae) live only in the New World. The greatest concentration of species and number of individuals is in Central America, in Colombia, Ecuador and Peru. Ecuador, the geographical centre of the group, has approximately half of the known species (130 out of 319). They are also found in the West Indies and Juan Fernandez, but are absent from the Galapagos. The majority of the species are static within this tropical belt; they are found at all altitudes on the mountains. There much of the terrain is marginal for their existence, and populations may be virtually confined to particular limited patches of forest on the hillsides. Some species have been found on the edge of the snow-fields and also in desert areas where their only food is the fruit and flower nectar of the Cacti (Berlioz, 1956).

A few migratory species range to the North and South of the main belt during the favourable season. *Eustephanus galeritus* was seen visiting *Fuchsia* flowers during a snowstorm in Tierro del Fuego. Two well-known Northern migrants are the Rufous humming-bird, *Selasphorus rufus* and the Ruby-throated humming-bird, *Archilochus colubris* L. The first penetrates up the West coast as far as Alaska, the second keeps more to the Eastern States and Canada and may reach Labrador. In both cases the birds travel more than 2000 miles from their winter quarters. In the spring, the Ruby-throated migrates gradually, following the movement northward of the 35°C isotherm, which leaves a trail of abundant spring flowers in its wake, on which the bird subsists. It arrives at its northern breeding ground about the middle of April. The journey south in the autumn precedes the first frosts which destroy its livelihood. The bird is, at the time of departure, exceedingly fat, having added 50 per cent to its normal weight in fat alone (Carthy, 1956). There is some evidence that it may fly nonstop across the Gulf of Mexico: this means 500 miles of continuous wing action, a tremendous achievement for a bird with a wing span of 4–4·75 in.

The Sun-birds, Nectarinidae, are restricted to the tropical and sub-tropical regions of the Old World. According to Delacour there are a hundred and four species. They are abundant in tropical and South Africa, and fifty-six species live in Eastern and N.E. Africa, but they are absent from the North West. About thirty species are found in S.E. Asia and Malaya. Eastwards they reach Queensland and Northwards, the Himalayas and South China. Like the Humming-birds, they cannot subsist on flower nectar alone and the protein in their diet comes from spiders, flies and beetles. They are *non-migratory*, but have to move about locally to follow flowers as they come into bloom. *Hedydipna platura*, the Pygmy sun-bird, does not seem bound by this necessity, for it leaves its breeding grounds just as the main tree, an *Acacia*, starts to flower.

Their habitats are similar to those of the Humming-birds for they are chiefly forest dwellers in the mountain ranges. Within the mountains they inhabit a variety of terrains. Some are alpine species, found up to the limits of vegetation, others do not penetrate above the subalpine zone. *Nectarinea famosa*, the Malachite sun-bird, and *N. johnstoni*, the Scarlet-tufted Malachite sun-bird, occupy a belt between 5500 and 14,000 ft. These are hardy little birds, undaunted by cold strong winds, the former living either on the moorland or in the bamboo zone; the latter chiefly on the moors where it roosts in holes in the matted dead leaves of the giant *Senecios* (Mackworth-Praed, 1955). *Cinnyris afer*, the great Double-collared sun-bird, keeps to the upper bamboo and tree heath zone on Mt. Ruwenzori, that is between 10,000 and 11,500 ft. *N. kilimensis*, the Bronze sun-bird and *Cyanomitre alinae*, the Blueheaded sun-bird, do not live above 6000 ft and chiefly forage *Erythrina* (Papilionatae) which occurs lower down. *Cinnyris bifasciatus*, the Little Purple-banded sun-bird, is abundant not only in the *Acacia* bush but also in the coastal mangrove swamps. *C. mariquensis*, the Mariqua sun-bird, a local species of *Acacia* scrub (an open association with short grass), subsists on insects in the grass heads when no nectar flowers are available. All these zones have their own particular flora and some species cannot exist without certain plants; for example *Anthobaphes violacea* and *Promerops cafer* only live in the *Protea* territory. They cannot adapt themselves to cultivated crops or exotics and leave any region where agriculture encroaches and displaces the *Protea*.

The Honey-eaters and Spinebills, Meliphagidae, are found throughout the S.W. Pacific but are chiefly concentrated in Australia and New Guinea. Some seventy of the hundred and sixty species are Australian and distributed from tropical North Queensland, down the eastern coast and around to South and South West Australia. As in the previous groups of birds, here again different species tend to occupy different territories and ecological associations. *Acanthorhynchus tenuirostris*, the Eastern Spinebill, frequents heathland and open forest; and *A. super-ciliosus*, the Western Spinebill, the *Banksia* (Proteaceae) country of S.W. Australia.

Myzomelia obscura, the Dusky Honey-eater, inhabits the coastal scrubs and Mangroves, and *Meliphago ornata*, the Mallee Honey-eater, the Mallee Scrub from N.W. Victoria to S.W. Australia. A New Zealand species, *Prosthemadera novae-zelandiae*, the Tui, is a forest bird, abundant in the North Island which migrates in early summer to the coast to exploit the Pohutukawa, *Metrosideros excelsa*.

The White-eyes, or Silver-eyes, Zosteropidae, are forest birds distributed throughout the tropics of the Old World. There are eighty-five species, and among the African members, there are many ecotypes, which adhere rather strictly to particular plant associations. Their chief food is insects, but they also eat fruit: they tend to peck flowers to obtain the nectar.

The Brush-tongued Lories and Lorikeets, Lorinae, are parrot like and found in Eastern Australia from Cape York to Victoria and Tasmania. They are particularly associated with the eucalypt forests but cover large areas in search of a succession of nectar flowers.

BODY STRUCTURE OF FLOWER-VISITING BIRDS

There is a superficial similarity between the Humming-birds and Sun-birds in the range of size, the shape of bill and the structure of the tongue (Berlioz, 1956). Here the likeness ceases, for they belong to quite different families as is apparent in their basic structure. The Sun-birds are **passerine** or perching birds; their wings are rounded and their feet strong and relatively long-boned. They alight on the stems when feeding and exploit the flowers either from above or below as is the most convenient for them. The Humming-birds perhaps show some alliance with the **picarian** birds, the Swifts, but they are really very isolated taxonomically. Their wings are oar-shaped and their feet very tiny, short-boned and with very sharp claws. No birds equal them in powers of flight: they can fly in any direction, rise vertically and fly backwards. The wing moves only at the shoulder joint and rather like an oar. The beat is virtually constant. The wings move in a horizontal plane while hovering, and in a nearly vertical plane when in top speed flight (Greenewalt, 1960). Both groups are small, ranging in size from that of a sparrow to a bumble-bee. *Calypte helenae*, a Cuban humming-bird, is tinier still, indeed, it is the smallest bird known. The male of *Calliphlox amethystina* weighs less than 1/10 oz.

The Brush-tongues, or Lories and Lorikeets, are a highly specialized race of parrots. The body is small and the powerful grasping feet enable the bird to cling in any position. The wings are long and the flight powerful. They can travel far in search of currently flowering trees. This is necessary, for tropical trees have very short blooming periods. The other groups of nectar feeders, the Meliphagidae, Zosteropidae and Drepanididae, are of small to medium size. They show no particular adaptation to flower feeding except in tongue and bill.

THE BILLS

In the Lories the bill is small, elongated and compressed laterally so that it easily enters the corolla. In the Humming-birds and Sun-birds, the bill, for the whole of its length, is very

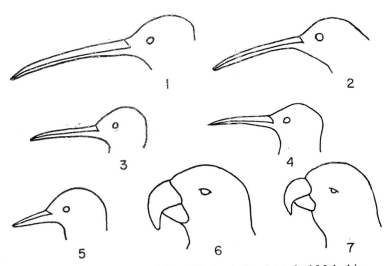

Fig. 37. Bills of flower-visiting Birds. 1. Scarlet tufted Malachite Sun-bird. *Nectarinea Johnstoni*, length 31 mm, and 2. West African Olive Sun-bird, *Cyanomitra divacea guineensis*, 24 mm, both Nectarinidae. 3 and 4, two unidentified Humming-birds, 23 mm and 19 mm: both Trochilidae. 5. Oriental White-eye, *Zosterops palpebrosa*, 12 mm, Zosteropidae. 6. Black capped Lory, *Domicella domicella*, upper mandible 23 mm, and 7. Red collared Lorikeet, *Trichoglossus rubritorques* upper mandible 20 mm; both Loriidae.

thin and narrow. In the Humming-birds it is very delicate in texture, with so little horn developed that it is at least partly flexible. Despite this, the needle-fine tip is quite firm and sometimes both the upper and lower jaws have serrations for 4–6 mm back of the tip which makes the bill a good holding tool for catching and dissecting prey. It is tubular: the lower mandible is "H"-shaped in section and fits up into the crescent shaped upper mandible leaving an almost square channel for the tongue. The shape varies from straight to curved: the direction of the curve is usually downward and may be slight or so strong that the bill is sickle-shaped. Lengths vary from 8–10 mm in the straight bill of *Microlyssa cristata* to 80–100 mm in *Ensifera ensifera* (Andean species) where it equals the body length and is upturned at the tip. In the Sun-birds the upper mandible only slightly overlaps the lower whose edges are elastic. Both upper and lower jaws are toothed from the tip backwards for 1/3–1/2 their length. In the Honey-eaters and Honey-creepers the bill is very varied in shape. It may be long, slender and curved or short. The jaws are serrated at the tip as in the Sun-birds (Fig 37).

THE TONGUES

The Lories' tongue is large and long and highly extensile and can be thrust deep into the flower. It has papillae, in the form of erectile fibres, on the distal part of the upper surface, which are arranged to fashion a double brush (Fig. 38). The Humming-birds' tongue is protrusile. It has a solid base, the **basihyal**, which is articulated with a bone, the **os entoglossum**, and then it divides into two "quills"—the slit in the quill being to the outer side in each case. Towards its end, each quill unrolls to give a fimbriated tip, the teeth of which point backwards. The articulation at its base helps it to function, the movement being brought about by two pairs of muscles, one pair protruding and the other pair retracting the tongue. The tubes of the quills end blindly in the basihyal and therefore do not connect with the bird's throat. The exact mechanism by which the tongue removes nectar from the flower is still in some doubt. It is not capable of sucking it up. The tongue oscillates rapidly in use and nectar flows into the *open* sides of the tubes, but it is not quite clear how it is transferred to the pharynx.

The tongues of the Sun-birds, Honey-eaters and Honey-creepers split distally into two tubes and may be fringed and frayed at the tip. They cannot be thrust out for more than 5–10 mm. The tubular part of the tongue fills automatically when protruded into liquid because of the vacuum which this action produces between its base and the palate. But here too, as in the Humming-birds, the cavities of the tube of the tongue sometimes fail to connect with the basal furrow which leads to the throat (pharynx). When in use "the tongue tip seems to oscillate at high frequency" (Melin, 1930), and this does not support the suggestion that it may be a **suctorial** organ. Melin thinks that the action is a combination of "wiping, lifting and pumping" both here and in the Humming-birds.

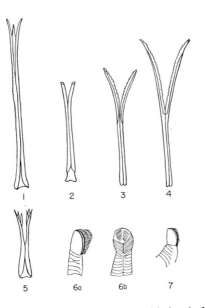

FIG. 38. Tongues of flower-visiting birds. 1. *Nectarinea Johnstoni*, length 36mm; 2. *Cyanomitra divacea guineensis*, 29mm; 3. and 4. two unidentified Humming-birds, 25 and 21mm; 5. *Zosterops palpebrosa*, 10mm; 6 a and b. *Domicella domicella*, 16mm; 7. *Trichoglossus rubritorques* 9·5mm.

THE SENSES OF FLOWER-VISITING BIRDS

SIGHT

The Humming-birds have very acute vision, as their darting direct flight to the flowers shows. They have been seen to fly over flowers and look into them, moving on if there is no nectar left in them. They are aware of bees visiting flowers and will follow their lead.

COLOUR SENSE

The Humming-birds have coloured oil drops in the retina of the eye. We do not know how this affects their colour vision. They are very sensitive to the long rays of the spectrum, i.e. the red and orange range, and are attracted by strongly saturated colours. They also visit yellow, white and violet and less often blue and green. The Honey-eaters in Australia freely visit red, cream, green and yellow flowers but never blue or brown (Sargent, 1928).

SENSE OF TASTE AND SMELL

The Humming-birds have taste-buds in the mouth, but there is no evidence so far that any of the flower-visiting birds have a sense of smell.

THE FEATURES OF BIRD FLOWERS

Birds visit such a variety of flowers that it is not possible to define a "bird" flower, but certain features tend to occur fairly frequently. The parts of the three continents which the birds inhabit have vastly different floras, and we find that the types of flower visited are just those which supply the most nectar in any given territory. *Copious* nectar is the primary feature of a bird flower. This may be supplied by many small flowers or large inflorescences or separate large flowers. Copious nectar needs a large container. The flowers are often large and fashioned as broad tubes (*Musa*, Fig. 36), and *Nicotiana glauca* (Fig. 39), narrow tubes (*Loranthus*) or funnels (*Hibiscus* and *Ipomea*). The Eucalypts (Gum Trees), *Metrosideros* (Rata) and *Callistemon* (Bottle-brush) all belonging to the Myrtaceae, have cup-shaped receptacles, often filled to overflowing. The tropical members of the Ericaceae have bell- or urn-shaped corollas, down the inside of which the nectar may form a big teardrop. The *Banksias* and *Grevilleas* (Fig. 26), belonging to the Australian branch of the Proteaceae, have stiff, erect brushes or sprays of small flowers and also in Australia are the sail-shaped flowers of *Clianthus* (Fig. 40) and *Templetonia* (Papilionaceae), where the standard is laid back in a straight line with the keel. The long flasks of the *Proteas* (Fig. 41) are composed of tightly

FIG. 39. *Nicotiana glauca*. Bird Flower. Tubular corolla, 38 mm long. The nectar rises 12 mm in the tube and contains 22 per cent sugar.

FIG. 40. *Clianthus dampieri*, Papilionaceae. Bird Flower. Attitude of flower presents no landing platform and standard petal is laid back until almost in line with the keel. Nat. size.

overlapping bracts which hold the nectar from the small central flowers. The whole inflorescence is held nearly upright and contains spoonfuls of nectar. *Mutisia* (Compositae) inflorescences look like *Fuchsia* flowers, both are bird-pollinated. The nectar is often rather weak, but varies widely in concentration depending on the species, for example, from *Callistemon*

FIG. 41. *Protea mellifera* inflorescence. Bird Flower. The small flowers are, at this stage, completely enclosed in the overlapping bracts which act as a nectar reservoir. ×0·33.

coccineus 13 per cent, *Musa velutina* 14 per cent, and *Leonotis leonurus* (Fig. 42) 20 per cent sugar to *Billbergia nutans* 30 per cent, *Lachenalia aloides* 39·5 per cent and *Abutilon striatum* 42 per cent sugar (Table 3). The bananas, *Musa* and their relatives, the Crane flower, *Strelitzia* and Traveller's Tree, *Ravenala* have slimy mucilaginous nectar. Each flower of *Billbergia* produces 40 mg of nectar, *Abutilon megapotamicum* 109 mg, *A. striatum* var. *Golden Fleece* 137 mg and *Musa*, male flowers 150 mg. These are modest amounts compared with the liqueur glass of nectar secreted by single flowers of the Spear Lily, *Doryanthes excelsa* (Jaeger, 1961).

There is a simplicity of design in many bird flowers, particularly in the Australian species. The petals and sepals are often strongly reduced in size and caducous. In *Beaufortia sparsa* they are only represented by scales. The "cap" of the *Eucalyptus* flower is thrown off as the flower opens. The Kangaroo Paws,

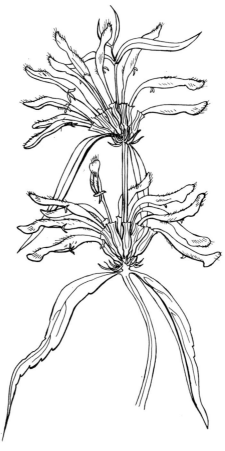

FIG. 42. *Leonotis leonurus*, Labiatae. Bird Flower. Part of inflorescence, ×0·5. Corolla delicate in texture, offers no landing platform, average amount of nectar per flower 17·5 mg, with 20 per cent sugar.

Anigozanthus spp. (Fig. 43) are also very simply constructed. The perianth is tubular at the base then splits and flattens at the end into the "paw" with its six pointed "claws" (the tips of the tepals).

Bird flowers are not orientated in any particular way; they may be erect, pendulous or patent. Neither is there a particular plane of symmetry as in bee flowers: few of them except the Salvias, Lobelias and the papilionate bird flowers are markedly zygomorphic, hence there is seldom a landing platform. Even

111

the papilionate flower is simpler in construction than the insect-pollinated species. There is no tripping mechanism and in *Erythrina indica* the keel is missing and the stamens and style freely exposed. The absence of a platform is scarcely a disadvantage, for the Humming-birds take the nectar while hovering

Fig. 43. *Anigozanthus flavidus*, Haemodoraceae, Kangaroo Paw. Bird flower of simple construction with no landing platform and semicircle of exerted stamens which come in contact with bird's head. Length of tube, 29 mm.

before the flower, and the Sun-birds can perch in any position and reach up or down into the flowers. *Strelitzia*, *Ravenala* and the Heliconias, however, have zygomorphic flowers and zygomorphic inflorescences. The plan of these three is similar. A large keel-shaped bract subtends one or more flowers, which, as they bloom appear up out of the bract in succession one after the other. In *Strelitzia*, each flower has three outer erect sepals which are regular. The inner whorl is irregular. Two of the petals form a long stiff spear-head which is hollow towards the base where the edges of the petals inroll and meet. In this hollow the stamens and style lie hidden and are only exposed by the pressure of the bird's body. The third petal is short and broad and blocks the entrance to the nectar cavity (Fig. 44).

FIG. 44. *Strelitzia reginae*, Strelitziaceae, The Crane Flower, bird pollinated ×0·3. Two flowers have emerged from the boat-shaped bract subtending the inflorescence. Two petals form a hollow spear head in which anthers and style are hidden. The third petal is short and blocks the entrance to the nectar cavity.

Three sepals stand erect and at right angles to the spear.

This barrier is firm and needs the strength of a Sun-bird to overcome it.

The stamens are often held well forward in the mouth of the corolla. In *Hibiscus* they form a strong central column terminating in a mop-head of anthers, in *Ipomoea* they form a central cone. The eucalypts and other Myrtaceae have a thick fringe of stamens surrounding the edge of the nectar cup.

The Humming-bird flowers are usually as delicate in structure and texture as hawkmoth or butterfly flowers. Many of those visited by Sun-birds (Nectarinidae) and Honey-eaters (Meliphagidae) are much stouter. Firstly, the stem of the inflorescence is strong and so are the pedicels of the flowers. The tissues of the flower and its bracts are either thick and turgid, as in *Musa* and *Protea*, or tough and coriaceous. The ovaries especially are protected from the birds' beaks, either by being enveloped in the bracts (*Heliconia*) or by a strong development in them of lignified tissue: "Gum nuts", *Eucalyptus* ovaries, are very hard even at flowering time. The styles are thick and rigid (*Grevillea*) or, if thin, woody and remarkably stiff and springy (*Banksia*). The filaments of the stamens are likewise strong and rigid, and the anther walls themselves may be almost woody.

Generally speaking, the bird flowers lack scent, but again there are many exceptions, one being *Serjania caracasana*, (Sapindaceae).

Vivid colours, highly saturated, characterize many bird flowers and probably these alone attract birds from a distance. Pure red, blue and green predominate. *Erythrina tomentosa*, *Manettia inflata* (Rubiaceae); *Metrosideros*, of New Zealand; *Callistemon coccineus*, *Lobelia cardinalis*, *Salvi splendens*, *Eucalyptus macrocarpa* and *Aloë excelsa* are red. The *Puyas*, *Tillandsia*, *Billbergia*, and *Bromelia*, all belonging to the Bromeliaceae are cobalt blue and green. There are many striking colour contrasts as well; orange and blue in the Crane Flower, *Strelitzia reginae*; green and scarlet in *Anigozanthus bicolor*, red and yellow bracts in *Protea mellifera*. Of the two Australian Pea Flowers, *Templetonia retusa* is red with a yellow "eye" and *Clianthus speciosus*, red with a black eye. The Lobeliaceae in Hawaii differ; 40 per cent have pink to purple flowers and 31·6 per cent have white flowers. Only 6·8 per cent are either red or yellow. Flower birds also visit small insignificant flowers with dull colours such as *Buddleia brasiliensis* (Loganiaceae) and *Hohenbergia angusta* (Bromeliaceae). There is a striking similarity of colouring between some Sun-birds and the flowers they visit. The male *Cinnyris senegalensis* has a brilliant scarlet breast which matches the colour of the buds of

Aloë excelsa. A scarlet patch on the breast occurs in the males of other species too.

Slimy, thready pollen is commonly found in the Bromeliads and their allies. In *Strelitzia reginae* there are sticky threads among the pollen grains which are derived from the cells of the anther wall: these, with hundreds of pollen grains attached to them, adhere to the breast or belly of the bird in long chains. In the Onagraceae (*Fuchsia* and *Oenothera*) the pollen is bound by viscin threads which enable hundreds of grains to be removed at a time. The Malvaceae have very tacky pollen: the grains are spiny coated and tend to cling together, as in *Hibiscus*. The acacias have compound grains and in the Ericaceae they are in tetrads, but these are more powdery in consistency. Many other bird plants have powdery pollen, so we cannot say that thready pollen is associated with bird pollination. Nevertheless it sticks readily to feathers.

THE BEHAVIOUR OF FLOWER-VISITING BIRDS

We have already seen that different species of flower birds, particularly the Humming-birds, tend to inhabit specific territories within their general range, and that these areas have distinctive plant associations. This is unlikely to be a direct link with the flowers as the animal food is the more important fraction of the birds' diet, and the terrain must of necessity, be favourable to the Arthropods. Yet, in their small local migrations the Nectarinidae follow the plants as they come into bloom. In Australia the Meliphagidae and Lories travel extensively in search of flowering trees.

Humming-birds and Sun-birds visit flowers continuously throughout the day, even during the hottest part. *Rhodopis vesper* flies in the evening and the Costa humming-bird continues its foraging into the night. They seldom touch the flower except with their bills; but Beebe (1950) has seen all the resident humming-birds, including *Aglaiocercus kingi-margarethae*, the Bronze-tail, at Portachuelo Pass, behaving quite abnormally. They were alighting on the plants, and, using both wings and feet, were scrambling over the leaves to work the flowers. As

115

the foliage was very damp, the birds too, became damp and dishevelled. They continued to do this for weeks on end, although they flew normally to pick spiders out of their webs as well. This curious behaviour is unexplained.

The Humming-birds show no marked flower constancy, although they tend to remain at an abundant nectar source. Nor are they colour constant: *Pygmornis* sp. flies from dull red *Hippotis brevipes* (Rubiaceae) to the whitish *Mendonica sp.* (Acanthaceae). They may have some appreciation of difference of colour shade, for the greenish young flowers of *Nicotiana glauca* (Fig. 30) are sometimes probed instead of the yellowish older flowers. They do not especially visit flowers with tube lengths matching the length of their bills. *Chlorostilbon aureiventris*, with a bill of 17–19 mm visits *Cestrum campestre* (Solananceae), whose flowers are the same length, *Serjania caracasana* with 10 mm flowers, and *Canna coccinea* with 30–40 mm tubes. There is no evidence that it pollinates any of these species.

The Humming-birds are the "bees" of the flower-bird world. Like the honey-bee they are highly adaptable and opportunist, quickly taking over new parks or garden territories, and utilizing any cultivated exotic. Short-billed species rob nectar by piercing corolla-tubes, just like the short-tongued bumble-bees on red clover. In Brazil they frequently steal from *Abutilon* and *Jacaranda* (Bignoniaceae), as does the biggest native bee, a *Xylocopa*. *Chlorostilbon aureiventris* is a secondary nectar thief, robbing through the holes made in *Tecoma* sp. tubes by *Xylocopa brasilianorum*.

The Sun-birds (Nectarinidae) take nectar without damaging the flowers if it is accessible, but, if it is beyond their reach, they become agressive and rip the corollas open.

Melianthus major has reddish purple flowers close set on the terminal 18 in. of a stout 4–5 ft inflorescence stalk. There is a large cup-shaped nectary at the lower side of the flower, enclosed in a blunt spurred sepal. It secretes abundant black nectar. The flowers are protandrous: first the upper, and then the lower pair of anthers are presented at the mouth of the flower for dehiscence; then they all bend outwards and the style elongates and moves downwards to take their place, and the stigmas open.

Nectarinea chalybea almost invariably exploits the flowers systematically working from the bottom to the top of the spike, its head feathers receiving and transmitting the pollen (Scott–Elliot, 1889). This method of working the inflorescence parallels the behaviour of the bumble-bees and is the most effective for cross-pollination of a spike of protandrous flowers (*see* Behaviour of Bumble-bees).

In the Australian Meliphagidae, flower constancy may be a necessity, as drought may seriously limit supplies. They, too, attack flowers with inaccessible nectar and cause severe damage to the urn-shaped corollas of the *Ericas* and the *Arbutus*. The Lories crush flowers and then lick up the nectar.

THE EFFICIENCY OF BIRDS AS POLLINATORS

More data are needed to assess the efficacy of the birds' flower visits. Some birds are completely dependent on certain flowers. The classic example is that of the sun-bird, *Promerops cafer*, which is only found in association with the Proteas (*P. mellifera*, *P. incompta*, *P. longiflora* and *P. scolymus*). The bird's beak and tongue are long and narrow, and the inflorescence is a narrow flask. Scott-Elliot (1889–90) considers it pollinates them effectively. In Natal, *Cinnyris olivaceous* and *Barbetula pusilla* pollinate *Loranthus kraussianus*, and *C. verreauxi* pollinates *L. dregei*. *Nectarinea souimanga* and *N. afra* respectively pollinate the Travellers' Tree, *Ravenala madagascariensis* and the Crane Flower, *Strelitzia reginae*. The birds easily probe the flowers with their curved beaks; the bees have difficulty in gaining access. In Natal, the bananas are bird-pollinated by species of *Cinnyris*, but in Mauritius they are insect-pollinated.

Among the Humming-birds, *Glancis hirsuta* and *Phaethornis guyi* pollinate *Centrogogon surinamensis* (Campanulaceae) in Trinidad. The curve of the beak matches that of the corolla and the pollen is dusted onto the forehead and head. The Ruby-throated humming-bird, *Archilochus colubris*, is the chief pollinator of *Impatiens capensis*, and also pollinates other species growing in North America such as *Tecoma radicans*, *Hibiscus lasiocarpus*, *Lobelia cardinalis*, *Gossypium herbaceum*, *Aesculus parviflora* and *Lonicera sempervirens*. It carries the pollen of the last species on the feathers at the corner of its mouth. The Solitary bees and honey-bee do not touch the anthers or stigma of *Impatiens capensis*, which lie against the roof of the flask-shaped corolla. The bird dislodges the pollen onto its head, and truly effects cross-pollination.

The Meliphagidae are efficient pollinators of *Eucalyptus calophylla*: the insects fail to touch the single stigma arising

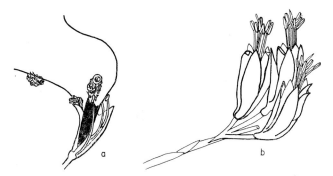

FIG. 45. a. *Prosthemadera novae-zelandiae*, The Tui, and *Phormium tenax*, the New Zealand Flax, showing the matching proportions of the bill and flower tube, the velvety feathers of the lores coming in contact with the anthers.
(Copied by kind permission of Mr. C. McCann from his original drawing.) Nat. size. b. *Phormium tenax*. The flowers stand nearly erect, the bird bending over to exploit them. ×0·5

from the centre of the receptacle cup, well separated from the fringe of stamens. The Honey-eaters visit the eucalypt forests in great flocks and cross-pollinate the flowers on the individual trees, but they only effect xenogamy to a limited extent, and this latter is more favourable to seed set. The White-plumed Honey-eater pollinates *Anigozanthos viridis* (Kangaroo Paw). The flower tube is slightly curved and split along its lower side. The anthers fringe the crescentic mouth of the tube and the stigma is also held back against it. The length and curve of both tube and beak match, and the forehead receives the pollen and also touches the stigma (Wakefield, 1960). The head and beak of the Tui, *Prosthemadera novae-zelandiae* shows a remarkable fit with the flowers of the New Zealand Flax, *Phormium tenax*. The feathers on the lores (the part of the face between the beak and the eye) are velvety and quite different from the rest of the feathers on the head, and may be a special adaptation for pollen collecting (McCann, 1952). (Fig. 45).

THE ADAPTATION OF BIRDS TO PLANTS

There is no fossil evidence of flower-visiting birds. Whether or not they are adapted to flowers is difficult to decide. The data has been extensively studied by Melin (1935), and he is of the opinion that, apart from the tongue, there is no unexceptional evidence of adaptation. He considers that the birds' specialized wings and beaks have previously evolved in connection with other activities, and that they are simply using these to exploit the flowers. So the bird–flower relationship is one of *utilization* of the flower by the bird and is not adaptive. These views are not shared by Porsch (1926) who likens the relationship between *Promerops cafer* and the Proteas to that between the long-tongued bumble-bees and *Aconitum*.

CHAPTER VII

POLLINATION BY BATS (Cheiropterophily)

OBSERVATIONS by McCann (1931) and Van der Pijl (1941) on the flower visits of bats proves that they are the pollinators of many species.

The bats are crepuscular or nocturnal and eat insects, flower petals, and fruit, as well as nectar and pollen. They are tropical: *Glossophaga soricina* Poll., a small new world species, and *Eonycteris* and *Macroglossus*, larger bats of the old world, have long slender muzzles and long pointed tongues which are highly extensile. The tip of the tongue has very fine papillae and these aid in sucking up the nectar. When drinking the tongue moves in and out very rapidly. They also eat large quantities of pollen, and Heide and Pijl consider the rasp-like tongue of *Eonycteris spelaea* Dobs, to be an adaptation for pollen collection. The dentition differs from that of the bats which mainly feed on insects, the front teeth being so small that they scarcely protrude through the gums.

They are proven to be colour-blind (Allen, 1939, cited Pijl), but pale colours, which are a feature of nocturnal flowers, should be visible to them.

FEATURES OF "BAT" FLOWERS

The flowers which bats visit have, over all, many similarities and it may be significant that these are all *positive* attributes, as are those of bee flowers. The chief of these have been enumerated by Pijl (1941).

The type of inflorescence is often **flagelliform**; that is to say the flowers, either in bunches, racemes, or even singly, dangle at the end of long leafless inflorescence stalks. The length of these may be quite phenomenal as in *Mucuna gigantea* where the ropelike stalks depend from trees 20 m in height to within 1–1·5 m of the ground, and even in less extreme cases suspend the flowers well away from branches and foliage. This should help the bats to see the flowers and also to land easily on them.

There are several types of flower form. Pijl draws attention to the fact that cheiropterophily is not an isolated phenomenon in tropical families, if it occurs in one branch it is apt to be present in several. He does not postulate any adaptation of the flowers to bats, but points out that the individual characters are found separately in many related species, and are only meaningful when they occur altogether in a single species, as in the leguminous *Mucuna Junghukniana*, which he considers to be a bat flower *par excellence*.

Kigelia pinnata (Bignoniaceae) has a flaring, relatively short-tubed corolla and is sufficiently commodious for the little bat to fold itself up neatly within it while drinking the nectar.

Mucuna reticulata, a legume, with the characteristic papilionate facies, could well be designated a large bee or bird flower. But it is subtly different in that the wing petals are dimpled and then bulge slightly on the outside. This bump forms an admirable handhold for the bat whose claw marks have been found in just this position. *Adansonia digitata* differs again. The flower is pendant and the ball of stamens and stigma is thrust well forward of the petals—nicely positioned to brush against the bat when it alights to drink the nectar which collects in the reflex of the petals above (Jaeger, 1961).

Musa textilis the Manilla Hemp, which is also cheiropterophilous, has an inflorescence which resembles a large pointed bud. It is made up of thick overlapping bracts, each of which has a double row of flowers in its axil. The flowers are male, female or hermaphrodite, tubular, and contain copious rather slimy nectar. Other positive attributes of bat flowers are common to nocturnal flowers in general. Firstly, the flowers only open

121

towards dusk and anther dehiscence also occurs at this time; as in Kigelia and *Musa textilis* (Nur, 1958). Nectar is present in the flowers by the time that they are open. Both nectar and pollen are abundant in cheiropterophilous species. The scent becomes apparent as the flower opens and has largely disappeared by next morning. Here, it is of a particular kind, being variously described as "disagreeable", "musty" or "resembling sour milk". This is very different from the delicate perfumes of many well known night flowers which attract moths. It may however, on analysis, prove different chiefly in strength and not in kind.

The pale colours usually exhibited by nocturnal flowers are also found in some bat-pollinated ones: *Adansonia digitata* the Baobab, is white, *Mucuna gigantea* yellow green, *Musa textilis* pale yellow. Lastly, the flowers are often ephemeral. If they fail to be pollinated during the night the *whole* flower is abscissed the next morning or during the following day. If they have been successfully pollinated, the petals and stamens fall, leaving the ovary, stigma and pedicel firmly attached to the inflorescence stalk.

Although these characters build up a rather definite pattern for bat-pollinated flowers, we still require to know which of them are the truly significant ones in the flower–animal relationship. Is the flower explored for nectar or pollen first without any regard to its other attributes, and do these latter subsequently become meaningful and built into a recognizable and memorable pattern by the bats? It would appear that a strong scent and pale colour would aid the animal in finding the flowers, but the latter cannot be essential, as McCann has pointed out that *Kigelia pinnata* is a deep red—the least "visible" colour in the dusk.

THE BEHAVIOUR OF THE POLLINATOR

McCann (1931) describes the visits of the Short-nosed Fruit Bat, *Cynopterus sphinx*, to *Kigelia pinnata*, the Sausage Tree. The bat alights and sticks its head well down into the corolla, presumably to drink the copious nectar. The dehisced anthers and stigma stand over the visitor which must touch them, if not with the head and back, then with the snout which is jerked upwards as the bat springs back into flight. Other visitors were *not* seen and the flowers *were pollinated* so the case in point seems proven; the bat is the agent. Porsch confirms this from observations on the same species in Java; and also adds three other Bignoniaceous species, *K. aethiopica*, *Crescentia cujete* and *C. alata*. Heide and Pijl both agree that the first of these three is visited by the bat *Eonycteris spelaea* Dobs but are of the opinion that pollen only is taken. But McCann notes that the animal would scarcely push its head right down into the flower if it were only collecting pollen.

In another paper McCann (1933) describes how the Flying Fox (*Pteropus giganteus*) pollinates *Grevillea robusta* in India. There the plant makes the best of both worlds as the flowers are open day and night and may be pollinated by diurnal as well as nocturnal animals. The flowers have none of the characters usually associated with cheiropterophily, and, as this species is not native, this case should be interpreted as chance utilization by the bat, albeit that pollination is effected.

CHAPTER VIII

POLLINATION BY INSECTS (Entomophily)

THE ANTHOPHILOUS INSECTS

There are three main classes of flower-visiting insects: The *Hymenoptera* (Social and Solitary Bees and Wasps); the *Diptera* (Flies); and the *Lepidoptera* (Butterflies and Moths). The outline of their classification is given in Table 5. They are structurally adapted (except in the case of certain flies and midges) to fit them for exploiting flowers. Modifications are to be found in the eyes, the structure of which will be considered in the section on vision, the legs, body covering, mouth parts, stomach and wings. The bees are specially adapted for collecting nectar and pollen.

THE COLLECTION OF POLLEN

Inadvertent transference of pollen from one flower to another is likely to occur if the body and legs of the visiting insect are hairy even if the insect is not actively collecting pollen. Many flies and butterflies transport the grains casually and the tiny midges, Mycetophilidae, which pollinate *Arum maculatum* may be seen with pollen lodged in the angles of the leg joints and scattered on the wings. Those insects which collect pollen to feed directly to their grubs, namely, the social bees, or to provision a burrow with a pollen pellet, that is, the solitary bees, are structurally adapted to perform this function. These are the most important flower visitors, for the active collection of pollen usually leads to pollination. The insects seldom clean their body hairs completely of pollen and this enhances their value as cross-pollinators.

TABLE 5. Main classes of Anthophilous insects

Hymenoptera	Vespidae	*Vespa*	Social wasps
		Colpa	} Solitary wasps
		Eumenes	
	Bombidae	*Bombus* (Bumble-bees)	} Social bees
		Apis (Honey-bees)	
	Colletidae	*Colletes*	
	Andrenidae	*Andrena* (Willow and Golden-rod bees)	
		Onagrandrena (*Oenothera* bees)	
		Halictus (Water lily bee)	} Solitary bees
		Halictoides (Pickerel-weed bee)	
	Panurgidae	*Panurgus*	
	Megachilidae	*Megachile* (Leaf-cutter bees)	
		Osmia	
	Xylocopidae	*Xylocopus* (Carpenter bees)	
	Anthophoridae	*Anthophora*	
Diptera	Chironomidae	*Chironomus* (Non-biting midges)	
	Mycetophilidae	(Fungus gnats)	
	Ceratopogonidae	(Biting midges)	
	Tabanidae	*Pangonia* (Horse flies)	
	Nemestrinidae	*Megistorhynchus*	
	Bombylidae	*Bombylius* (Bee flies)	
	Syrphidae	*Syrphus* (Hover flies)	
		Eristalis (Drone flies)	
Lepidoptera	Nymphalidae	*Vanessa* (Tortoiseshells, Peacocks)	
		Pyrameis (Painted Lady)	
		Heliconius (Erato butterflies)	
		Danaus (Milkweed butterfly)	
	Sphingidae	*Herse* (Convolvulus Hawkmoth)	
		Deilephila (Striped Hawkmoth)	
		Macroglossa (Humming-bird Hawkmoth)	
	Noctuidae	*Barathra* (Cabbage moth)	
		Triphoena (Yellow Underwing)	
		Pluisa (Silver Y).	

125

FIG. 46. Hind leg of *Bombus terrestris*. a. Hairy femur; b. flattened tibia fringed with hairs = the corbicula or pollen-basket. c. Planta, the broad basal joint of the tarsus (foot) covered with stiff hairs = the pollen brush. ×6.

MODIFICATIONS FOR THE COLLECTION OF POLLEN

Insects collect pollen on their body hairs and legs. From the point of attachment to the tip, the leg consists of a basal joint (**coxa**) hinged to the body; a second small joint (**trochanter**), also hinged so that it can move vertically; a large thigh joint (**femur**), a shin joint (**tibia**), and lastly a five-jointed foot (**tarsus**) of which the basal joint (**planta**) adjoining the tibia is as large as the other four put together (Fig. 46). This generalized structure is modified in various ways in the different genera of bees.

POLLEN-COLLECTING APPARATUS OF THE HONEY-BEE

The planta of both the first and second pairs of legs is covered with long unbranched hairs which form a pollen brush for cleaning the foreparts of the body. Both the tibia and the planta of the hind pair of legs are wide and flat. In the former, the outer side is smooth and polished and fringed with long hairs. This is the **corbicula** or pollen basket. The inner surface of the latter (the planta) possesses ten rows of stiff hairs. This is a pollen brush used for cleaning the hind part of the body, but its chief function is to take pollen from the brushes on the middle leg and hold it ready for packing into the corbicula. Two more essential features are present, a pollen comb of stiff spines (pecten) at the end of the tibia and on its inner side, and a lip (auricle) which projects from the base of the planta where it abuts on the sloping end of the tibia.

Packing the pollen basket. With a downward movement the pecten of the right leg scrapes the tacky pollen from the planta of the left leg, filling the gap between its comb and auricle with pollen. Then the pecten of the left leg performs a similar movement. The planta joints now straighten, pressing the auricles against the end of the tibia. This action compresses the pollen and forces it upwards and on to the lower end of the smooth concave floor of the corbicula. The hind legs work alternately and successive pats of pollen are fed into the basket and the mass moves forward and upward. As the load increases in size, it is patted and shaped by the middle legs. The corbicula of the honey-bee has a special feature, a curved hair situated near the lower end of the bracket and pointing downwards. This is the anchoring post around which the load is built up until it bulges from the corbicula (Fig. 47). The pressure of the pollen on the hair pushes it into an upright position but it holds firm.

The nature of the hairs on the legs has a direct bearing on the type of pollen which is collected; indeed, some of the most delicate and precise relationships between flower and bee depend

127

on this feature alone. The honey-bee is able to pack the slightly tacky pollen of many temperate region flowers with ease and rapidity forming a neat and compact load. When however, it attempts to exploit the Evening Primrose (*Oenothera* spp.) it

FIG. 47. *Apis mellifera*, honey-bee worker with pollen load bulging from the corbicula. Medium length tongue (out of focus). ×7·5.

finds the big triangular grains with their sticky viscin threads quite intractable. It may amass a load but the pollen will not stay properly in the basket and "concertinas" out again, so that during the return flight, two ribbons of pollen stream out behind the bee. The true pollinators of *Oenothera* are the Onagrandrenas. The hairs of the tibia in these species are long and soft (Fig. 48) and the bees have no difficulty in packing the pollen expeditiously and tidily (Fig. 49). The degree of specialization of the tibial hairs is very high, the length of the hairs matching the size of the pollen grain collected. The hairs fringing the pollen basket of *Onagrandrena linsleyi* are longer but less dense,

F IG. 48. *Onagrandrena linsleyi,* showing the long soft hairs on the tibia which enable the bee to collect *Oenothera* pollen successfully. × 6.

than those of *O. rozeni* and *O. rubiotincta,* and it collects the pollen of *Oenothera deltoides.* This species has larger grains than either *Oenothera clavaeformis* or *Oenothera brevipes pallidula* which the two latter bees with their shorter hairs forage exclusively (Linsley and MacSwain, 1955).

The bumble-bees' (*Bombus*) pollen-collecting apparatus is essentially the same as that of the honey-bee except for two minor differences. Firstly, there is no anchoring hair on the floor of the pollen basket, and secondly, the hairs of the planta are scattered over its whole surface (instead of being in rows) (Fig. 46).

The hive- and bumble-bees are specially adapted to nototribic flowers such as the Labiates which deposit pollen on their backs (Figs. 5 and 50). *Megachile* and *Osmia* have no corbiculae.

FIG. 49. *Onagrandrena linsleyi* with a load of *Oenothera* pollen which it collects exclusively. × 6. The triangular shape of the individual grains is distinguishable.

Instead they have an *abdominal* pollen brush. In Osmia each segment carries a transverse row of long smooth hairs; in *Megachile* (Fig. 51), the whole underside of the abdomen is thickly covered by long spirally twisted hairs. These bees chiefly exploit sternotribic flowers such as Papilionates (Fig. 52) and Pycnostachys (Fig. 53), i.e. those in which the anthers come in contact with their bellies as they enter. They collect the pollen by expanding and contracting the abdomen.

In *Anthophora* the pollen is collected on the tibia and planta of the hind legs which have long, strong, smooth hairs on their outer, forwardly-directed sides.

The Carpenter bees (*Xylocopa*) have no highly developed pollen baskets for they swallow down large amounts of pollen into their crops and later disgorge it to form pellets to prime their larval tunnels, which they excavate in solid wood. The body and all the legs are very hairy and they brush pollen from

FIG. 50. *Lamium album*, a noto-tribic bumble-bee flower. The four anthers and stigma are housed in the upper lip of the corolla, the lower lip forming a landing plat-form. Total length of corolla 2 cm, corolla tube 9·5 mm.

their body hairs with the middle pair of legs, transferring it to the hind legs during flight.

Halictus, *Colletes* and *Panurgus* collect their pollen dry. There is no pollen basket as such: the pollen adheres thickly to the specially long crimped or feathered hairs of the hind legs.

Verbenajus verbenae (Panurgidae) is an oligolectic bee which collects solely from three species of Verbena, *V. hastata*, *V. stricta* and *V. urticifolia*. These flowers have the anthers

131

Fig. 51. *Megachile* sp. The abdominal brush is thickly coated with pollen. ×7·5.

included in the narrow-tubed corolla; and the bee extracts the pollen by inserting its front tarsi into the tube and drawing it up with its curled spines (Robertson, 1922).

MODIFICATIONS FOR COLLECTING NECTAR

MOUTHPARTS

We know very little of the history of development of these organs. The earliest example of an insect with piercing and suctorial mouthparts is *Eugereon boeckingii* Dohrn, from the Lower Permian of Germany (approx. 192 million years old). It is an impression on the rock surface of the head and thorax, and two slender blades appear fully extended in front of the head, and by their similarity with modern insects may be recognized as part of a suctorial proboscis. On this evidence the class of *Protohemiptera* was created. The Hymenoptera date from the

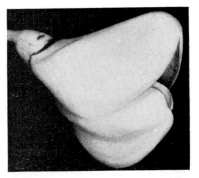

Fig. 52a. *Sarothamnus scoparius*, sternotribic pollen flower. Flower ready for exploiting, the stamens dehisce in the bud stage. ×2·5.

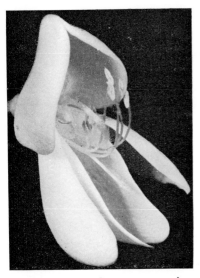

Fig 52b. *Sarothamnus scoparius*, sternotribic pollen flower. Flower after tripping. The stamens have sprung erect and the style has re-coiled back into the standard. ×2·5.

Jurassic (144 million years) but the Lepidoptera do not appear before the Tertiary (60–28 million years). The tertiary fossils, however, are highly organized members of their class, so the origin of the group must be much earlier. The Cretaceous rocks (92 million years) furnish our first records of angiosperm flowers, and these include not only willows and magnolias but such advanced types as *Dalbergia*, which is a papilionate flower.

FIG. 53. *Pycnostachys urticifolia*, Labiatae. Sternotribic bee flower. Top lobe of corolla small and stamens and stigma housed in lower lip. × 9.

Papilionate flowers today are closely associated with the long-tongued bees and butterflies, and it is difficult to believe that these were not present in Cretaceous times. Records of bees are lacking until the Tertiary; a *Megachile*, together with the leaves cut by it has been found in the Florissant shales, which are Miocene in age.

The proboscis of the honey-bee consists of a long slender hairy tongue or **glossa**, flanked on either side by two jointed **labial palps** and also by two long shining smooth blades,

134

concave on their inner faces, which are the **maxillae**. The margins of the tongue are curled inwards on the lower side and almost meet, forming a somewhat flattened tube. There is a tiny flexible spoon shaped lobe at the tip of the tongue. When about to drink, the labial palps and the maxillae close in around the tongue, forming an outer tube while leaving it (the tongue) free to move inside. The bee pushes its proboscis into the nectar until the tips of the maxillae are below the surface, then the tongue slides rapidly in and out past the end of the stationary maxillae and the nectar flows up, and, aided by the suction of the powerful muscles of the pharynx, enters the mouth. The honey-bee also has mandibles with which to manipulate solid food but these are incapable of biting through flower petals. The bumble-bees have stronger mandibles which easily nip holes in flower tubes and *Bombus mastrucatus* can pierce them with its proboscis alone.

The proboscis of the solitary bee, *Andrena*, is essentially similar in construction to that of the honey-bee, but it is much shorter, 2·7 mm as compared with 6 mm in the honey-bee, and the tongue is a broad hairy lobe. In between these two come *Megachile*, 4·1 mm and *Osmia*, 4·8 mm. There is some variation in the different races of honey-bee. Alpatov (1929) finds that in European Russia the length of the tongue varies with latitude, from 5·726 mm in the North to 6·733 mm in the South. The long-tongued bees are, *Xylocopa*, 8·4 mm; *Anthophora* 9·3 mm; and *Bombus*; from 8·2 mm in *B. terrestris* to 13·7 mm in *B. hortorum*.

Butterflies and moths have no mandibles and the long suctorial proboscis is formed from the two immensely elongated maxillae, each of which has a groove along its inner face. They are held close against one another by interlocking spines so that together they form a tube through which nectar is sucked. The proboscis is curled up like a watch spring when not in use (Fig. 54).

The flies, like the butterflies have no mandibles and only incompletely developed maxillae. The **labium** or tongue together with the **hypopharynx** (absent in the honey-bee), forms the proboscis and is widened and two-lobed at the tip. In the midges these lobes or **labellae** remain separate, but in the

FIG. 54. Head of *Herse convolvuli*, the Convolvulus Hawkmoth, with the tongue at rest, coiled like a watch spring. × 12·5.

Syrphids (Horse Flies and Drone Flies) they are partly fused. The surface of the labellae towards their end is covered by a thin membrane which contains many fine channels through which liquid food is sucked in. The delicate walls of the food channels are supported and kept open by ribs of chitin. When drinking the lobes are applied as a suctorial pad to the wet surface. In order to eat pollen, the labellae reflex strongly and expose minute prestomal teeth which rasp off and pulverize the grains. The food is then sucked directly into the mouth. The tongue length varies with the species; it is only 3 mm in *Syrphus ribesii*, a common species of Hoverfly, and 7 mm in *Eristalis tenax*, a Drone fly (Fig. 55). In the Bee-flies, *Bombylius*, all the mouthparts, including the labellae are extremely elongated and together form a slender proboscis which is not hinged at the base and so cannot be retracted. It sticks out like a fine needle in front of the head (Fig. 56). It is 1 cm long in *Bombylius major*, the pollinator of the primrose.

FIG. 55. *Eristalis tenax*, Drone Fly. Note proboscis terminates in a broad disc. The body and legs are hairy. ×6·5.

THE HONEY STOMACH

The honey- and bumble-bees are the only social insects which take nectar in excess of their individual requirements. They have a honey-stomach. This is a thin walled sac, flat and flabby when empty, but capable of great distension. In it they store the nectar they swallow and they also have the power of regurgitating it. While it is in the stomach, the nectar is mixed with the digestive enzyme, invertase, which converts it into honey. This capacious honey-stomach is a positive structural attribute which is valuable, not only to the bee, but to the plant, for many flowers can be visited and cross-pollinated in a single foraging flight.

WINGS

The Hymenoptera (bees) and Lepidoptera (butterflies) have two pairs of wings. The forepair interlocks with the hind pair, so that they work as one. The Diptera (flies) have one

137

FIG. 56. *Bombylius major*, Bee-fly with non-retractile proboscis, the pollinator of the primrose, *Primula vulgaris.* × 3·75.

pair of wings, the second pair being modified into small clubs, **halteres**, which by their vibration serve as balancers during flight. For the mechanism of wing movements the reader is referred to Wigglesworth's *Principles of Insect Physiology*. All these classes of insect are capable of strong and sustained flight which has an important bearing on their usefulness as pollinators. The habit of flight is also of importance in the flower relationship. Hovering is a marked feature of the flight of hawkmoths, hoverflies and bees, and also of that of the remarkable long-tongued flies, *Pangonia* and *Megistorhynchus*. The former classes hover in front of the flower, and the hawkmoths can exploit flowers with no landing platform: the latter hover above the flower in order to dip their slender pendant tongues into the erect corolla tubes.

INSECT SENSES

VISION

The compound eye is the chief organ of sight in the adult insect. The ocelli, the three simple eyes on top of the bee's head, perceive small changes in light intensity and enable the bee to respond rapidly to them. The resolving power of the compound eye depends on the number of its facets, the greater the number, the better the resolution. The House Fly, *Musca domestica*, has 4000, the honey-bee 3000–6000 and butterflies from 12,000 to 17,000. The visual acuity, i.e. the distinctness of vision, of a bee's eye has been estimated at about 1/50–1/100 of that of man in the vertical direction in good illumination. In poor light the resolving power is very low. Translating this into the familiar form of the oculists' test type, and taking the better figure of 1/50, it means that the largest letter would be legible at 2 ft and the smallest at 2 in. The largest letter would be invisible beyond 10 ft and the smallest beyond 10 in. A large buttercup, if showing as much contrast with the foliage as white does on black, would be visible to the bee at a distance of 5–6 ft.

The retinal image of the compound eye is a mosaic of points of light. Bees and butterflies respond to any change in this pattern and therefore are able to perceive *forms*. The honey-bee's degree of perception is not very great; it cannot distinguish between a square, disc or triangular shape. Bees trained to visit a saucer of syrup placed on a disc, will visit the other two shapes just as freely in search of food. Any figure with arms, such as a cross or "Y", or a more complicated rayed *flower-like* pattern is visited in preference to one of simpler outline. Bees can be trained to recognize and distinguish between a pattern of radiat, ing blue and yellow rays, which approximate to a daisy in form—and one of separate blue or yellow arms radiating from a centre which resembles a cabbage or gentian flower. The richer the contour, the more attractive is the shape to both butterflies and bees. Wigglesworth (1939) says "It would seem that the choice of forms by these insects is dependent merely on the frequency of change of retinal stimulation; and that they cannot recognize figure by any properties of configuration. In other words, that

139

the perception of form is little more than a perception of different degrees of flicker." He also remarks that bees settle more rapidly on flowers if they are being shaken by wind. The richest flower outlines are found in the climax groups of the Compositae, Scrophulariaceae, Labiatae, Papilionaceae, and Orchidaceae, which we particularly associate with these two groups of insects.

In the moth's eye, instead of the retinal or sense cell receiving only one point of light from a single facet, it receives light impinging on and reflected off the inner walls of several facets. This increases the luminosity of the image at the expense of its sharpness which is probably an advantage to a crepuscular insect. Hawkmoths (Sphingids) certainly perceive floral shapes for they will fly to flowers on patterned wall paper and attempt to exploit them. Flies perceive liquid-looking shiny surfaces such as the staminodes of *Parnassia palustris* which end in small knobs resembling drops of golden liquid. They also react to any moving or fluttering part of a flower. Recently, Burkhardt and Wendler (1960) claim to have proved directly that a single ommatidium (one of the visual elements comprising the compound eye) of *Calliphora erythrocephala* (the Blue-bottle) is capable of analysing the plane of polarization of polarized light.

Colour vision is well developed in bees and butterflies. We owe this knowledge to the ingenious experiments of Von Frisch (1950) who trained bees to visit coloured strips of paper. A blue paper was placed among thirty shades of grey paper (white to black) with a watch glass of sugar syrup on the blue slip as an attraction. The bees were allowed to visit it for 2 days. After this period of training the sugar was removed and the slips covered with glass to guard against the possibility of the papers smelling different. The position of the slips was altered, but no matter in what place it appeared, the bees always returned to the blue slip, showing that they distinguished it from any shade of grey. When trained to a yellow slip among the greys, a similar result was obtained. When however the bees were trained to a red slip they subsequently settled on red, black and dark grey—this indicates that the bee cannot see red. Further experiments were made to discover whether bees could distinguish one colour from another. If they were trained to blue and then presented with slips of all colours of the rainbow, they alighted on blue, purple and violet, evidently being unable to distinguish between these three shades. Similarly, after training to yellow they visited yellow, yellow-green and orange. These shades, distinct for us are concolorous for the bee.

Later work by Kuhn and Pohl using spectral light, established that bees perceive wavelengths from 300 $\mu\mu$ to 650 $\mu\mu$. Within this range, they distinguish only four bands: yellow to yellow-green (650–500 $\mu\mu$); blue-green (500–480 $\mu\mu$); blue (480–400 $\mu\mu$) and ultraviolet (400–300 $\mu\mu$). The bee cannot see the longer red rays (greater than 650 $\mu\mu$), it is "colour-blind" for red. The yellow-green band is the most attractive to bees and this is near to the region of the spectrum which appears brightest for man, but no colour is sought out by a honey-bee until it is recognized as having an association with food and learnt and integrated into a foraging pattern.

Many so-called "bee" flowers are yellow, blue or purple. It is also interesting to note that coloured nectar guides on petals always form a recognizable contrast for the bee's eye. In Forget-me-not it is yellow an blue, Ivyleaved Toadflax (*Cymbalaria muralis*) yellow on violet; Eyebright (*Euphrasia*) yellow on white. Out of ninety-four European flowers, thirty-three showed a yellow-blue contrast for the bee and twenty-nine a white-blue one.

Lutz and Richtmyer, by employing a direct vision spectroscope and also by photography through ultraviolet, red and blue filters, found that yellow petals and many red and blue petals reflect ultraviolet strongly, whereas the reflection from white petals is very slight. This explains why bees visit poppies. *Portulaca* and *Zinnia*, both of which look red to us, should easily be distinguished by bees, for the former reflects ultraviolet strongly and the latter does not. *Trigona* bees distinguish a pattern of Chinese white on white, when the latter reflects ultraviolet for the former does not.

Recent experiments by Daumer (1958) prove that the honey-bee's colour vision is much more definitive than had previously been realized. Working with mixtures of spectral colours, he finds that within the yellow range bees can, in some measure, distinguish orange, 616 mμ, yellow, 588 mμ and green 530 mμ. At the other end of the spectrum they distinguish between blue, 474 mμ and blue-violet 440 mμ, and also see two ultraviolets; u.v. 375 mμ and u.v. 360 mμ.

Daumer also defines two new colours for bees, **bee purple**, which is a mixture of yellow 588 mμ and u.v. 360 mμ, and **bee violet** a mixture of blue violet 440 mμ and u.v. 360 mμ. Within the bee-purple range, the bees can distinguish several shades, depending on the proportion of yellow to u.v. in the mixture. Two shades they distinguish clearly and another five moderately well. Within the bee-violet range, they distinguish no less than ten shades, three of them very well and seven moderately well.

Cabbage butterflies and the Orange Tip (Pierids), and also the Tortoiseshells (Vanessids), have a wider range of colour vision than the bees, for they can see red. They have, moreover, definite colour preferences. Ilse (1928) found that when Pierids were offered differently coloured papers they were attracted chiefly to red and purple, but the Vanessids (Tortoiseshell, Peacock, Painted Lady and Red Admiral) went to yellow and violet.

Colour memory. Honey-bees, after only 2 hours' training to a colour will remember it for 4 days. In comparison with bees, butterflies have poor colour memories, they forget a colour after 1 day, even though their previous training to it lasted 4 days.

SENSE OF TASTE

The sense of taste and the sense of smell are both chemical stimuli and difficult to separate from one another. Bees, which have sensory pits at the base of the tongue, can distinguish between sweet, bitter, salt and acid, but only nine sugars appear sweet to them as against thirty-four for human beings. These include the common sugars found in nectar such as sucrose, glucose, fructose and raffinose.

The threshold for perception of cane sugar is from 1 M to M/8 and is affected by the previous level of sugar feeding and the age of the bee, the older ones being less sensitive to sweetness. Butterflies show far greater sensitivity: the taste buds on the feet of a long-starved Red Admiral will detect an M/12,800 dilution of cane sugar and cause it to unroll its proboscis. Bees, too, detect greater dilutions of sugar with their tarsal taste organs than with their mouth parts. The greater the concentration of sugar, the more eagerly the bees drink it, and the greater is the vigour of the bee's dancing on its return to the hive. In the field the bees' flower visits are strictly controlled by the concentration of the nectar available (Chapter V).

SENSE OF SMELL

Insects are very sensitive to volatile substances which may be perceived by sensory pits on the legs and body as well as by the antennae. The antennae are chiefly concerned with the perception of scent. The sensory region is located in the last eight joints of the bees' antennae. Bees deprived of their antennae no longer respond to a specific odour to which they have been trained in association with their food.

The honey-bee's sense of smell is much the same as that of man. Flowers odourless to us are so to the bee. We cannot distinguish between the smell of nitrobenzol and bitter almonds, neither can the bee. The threshold of perception of flower scent for honey-bees and man is of about the same order of magnitude. Bumble-bees, however, are able to perceive the scent of Yellow Toadflax (*Linaria vulgaris*) and Viper's Bugloss (*Echium vulgare*) (Free, 1961). These are scentless to most humans.

The honey-bee is able to distinguish a particular scent in a mixture better than man. When trained to visit a dish of syrup scented with oil of orange, which was subsequently "hidden" by placing it among dishes scented with forty-three other ethereal oils, the bees unerringly selected the training scent. Bumble-bees have been trained to recognize *two* different scents at a time and then to pick both out from a selection of other perfumes. The honey-bees' own scent, which they can extrude by exposing the Nassonoff scent-organ situated on the front of the seventh segment of the abdomen, is powerfully attractive to their hive mates. There is evidence that they use this to mark the site of the crop on which they are foraging as a guide to other recruits.

The Carpenter bees (*Xylocopa*) have a strong and disagreeable body scent and it is employed by them in exactly the opposite way to that of the honey-bee. If it is present on the petals, it acts as a signal to the other foragers that the flower has been recently visited, and they sheer off in search of other blooms. This is advantageous for both insect and plant: the former is able to collect a load more rapidly and with less effort, and a higher proportion of the flowers of the latter will be visited.

Scent memory. The honey-bee has a tenacious memory for scent and will remember a training scent even after a lapse of several weeks.

INSECT BEHAVIOUR IN RELATION TO FLOWERS

It is now necessary to see how the anthophilous insects employ their senses to further their own economy and to see if we can find out how their patterns of foraging are built up and how these affect the pollination potential of the flowers they visit.

COMMUNICATION AMONG BEES

The bee dances. The honey-bees alone communicate information about their foraging experiences to their hive mates. Even the highly sophisticated bumble-bees do not appear to be able to match them in this. We owe our information on this to the classic researches of Von Frisch (1950).

When a honey-bee returns to the hive with a stomachful of concentrated nectar, it will first empty its crop and then run up onto the vertical face of the comb and begin to dance.

The round dance. If the bee has been foraging near to the hive the so called "round" dance is performed. The bee runs quickly, describing a tight circle, then just as it is about to complete the loop, it turns quickly about and runs back along its original circular path. When it reaches the top of the loop for the second time, it again turns and retraces its steps as before. This circular movement is often very rapid and is danced on a minimum area. During the dance, some of the neighbouring bees on the comb will face the dancer and touch her with their antennae, and perceive the scent of the flowers clinging to the body hairs of the forager. After perhaps half a minute, the dancer will shift its position and dance on another part of the comb face. Eventually it cleans its antennae, and leaves the hive to forage again. The round dance is performed when the bee has been foraging for pollen or nectar up to 50 m distance from the hive and is followed by the recruited bees searching all points of the compass in the near neighbourhood.

The waggle-tail dance. Returning from a distance of a 100 m, a different dance is performed, the so-called "waggle-tail" dance. The dancer describes what is essentially a figure-of-eight pattern, but the "waist" of the eight is broad and is called the "straight run". It is as if the pattern of the round dance had been stretched out into two circles instead of one. While travelling along the straight run, the bee wags its abdomen from side to side, hence the name given to the dance. This dance, by an alteration of its rhythm, indicates the *distance* of the food from the hive. If this is 100 m, the bee makes an average of eleven straight runs every 15 sec, if 300 m, an average of 7·6 runs; if 1000 m, 4·5 runs and 1500 m, 4 runs. Although the number of straight runs decreases with distance, the tail wags speed up. At 100 m there are two to three waggles per straight run; at 300 m, five to six; at 700 m, ten to eleven. The dance then does not lose any of its liveliness with increasing distance.

The waggle-tail dance also indicates the *direction* of the food source with great accuracy. Should the food be between the hive and the sun, the bee orientates its dance so that the straight run is performed by running vertically *up* the comb. Should the hive be between the sun and the food, the bee, on the straight run, runs vertically down the comb. Should the food-place form an angle with the sun and the hive, the bee inclines its waggle-tail run at exactly the same angle to the vertical as the source makes with the hive and the sun and either to left or right of the sun. Naturally, as the sun moves through the sky, the angle of the straight run also alters.

Bees perform the waggle-tail dance not only on the vertical combs but also on the horizontal surface of the alighting board. In this case the dancer does not orientate herself with the vertical, but points her waggle-run straight towards the food source.

If the angle of the straight run on the *vertical* comb is watched throughout the day, it is found that the bees appear to give false directions by *underestimating* the angle at which the food lies in relation to the sun in the morning, and *overestimating* it in the afternoon. This is true only if the food source lies due South of the hive. If the source lies to the East, they make too small an angle from 9 to 11 a.m., and 12.30 to 2.30 p.m., and too large an angle between 11 and 12.30 p.m. and 2.30 to 5 p.m. Yet the recruited bees arrive at the correct place. This means that the dancer's way of indicating angles is not quite the same as man's (Von Frisch, 1960).

The bee-dances continue even if the sun is obscured by thick cloud cover. They are still able to see the sun because of the extreme sensitivity of their eyes to ultraviolet rays.

When a hive of bees was placed in a big muslin cage, the bees did not dance, but if even a small hole was cut in the muslin through which the blue sky could be seen, the bees danced. This led Von Frisch to postulate that the bee's compound eye is sensitive to the plane and degree of polarization of the light from the blue sky. Each part of the blue sky reflects light which is polarized in a greater or lesser degree. The sky near the sun reflects non-polarized light. At the horizon the light reflected is completely polarized and there is a fairly regular change in the degree of polarization between these two extremes. If the bee's eyes can appreciate these differences then it will be able to orientate itself even if the sun is obscured. Recent work proves Von Frisch's hypothesis to be entirely correct.

An important feature of this "language" of the bees is that the vigour of the dance is proportional to the richness of the food, and a lively dance attracts more workers to the crop which has adequate food to offer, but may have unfortunate consequences for pollination if the nectar concentration of the flowers is low (see Chapter V).

FLOWER FORM

The *pattern* of the Angiosperm flower is very old and was present in the Jurassic Bennettitales, 135 to 180 million years ago. These gymnosperms had exactly the same sequence of parts on the reproductive axis as have flowers today. First came a ring of hairy bracts resembling a perianth, then a circle of curious pinnate stamens. Finally, tipping the axis, was a cone of stalked orthotropous ovules, whose long slender micropyles peeped out from between the peltate heads of stalked scales, which formed an almost continuous casing over them and performed the function of the ovary wall in the Angiosperms.

This pattern seems to have disappeared when the Bennettitales became extinct, and only very recently (geologically speaking), in the cretaceous age, 92 million years ago, did it reappear as the dominant flower form in the modern Angiosperms.

The flower form is realized in many different ways. The "form" has been called immortal, the means by which it is attained, transitory. It is the unit which the pollinating animal recognizes and this is not necessarily a single flower botanically. It may be achieved by a single flower, as in the buttercup, or by a capitulum, as in the daisy; or by a part of a flower as in the Iris. The last appears as three separate flower forms to the bee, each of which has to be exploited separately. In the Compositae even more complicated flowerlike units exist, where several capitula which have disc florets only, are grouped to fashion the centre of the "daisy", while other capitula of rayed florets surround them to give the daisy "petals". So our "flower" is an inflorescence of inflorescences.

In *Dorstenia* (Moraceae), the inflorescence axis itself assumes a flower-like appearance. The real flowers are minute and sunk into the fleshy central disc (Fig. 57).

APPRECIATION OF FLORAL FORM

Manning (1958), working with large flat discs of paper to represent flowers, finds that bumble-bees are firstly attracted by the contrast in colour made by the "petals" against their background. The bee alights nearer to the edge of the petals and only later examines the centre of the "flower". When the models were marked with a pattern simulating nectar guides, the bees did not react to the latter until they were actually hovering in front of the model. They flew equally freely to marked and unmarked models from a distance of 60 cm, the point at which they first become aware of the shape. This then may be the moment when the nectar guide on a petal becomes meaningful and helps to direct the questing bee. Scent gradients, or a different scent on one part of the corolla, as have been demonstrated by Lex (1954), may also assist. Anything suggesting depth in the model, such as a dark mark in the centre, or a

Fig. 57. *Dorstenia contrajerva*, Moraceae. The inflorescence axis mimics a flower-like form. The individual flowers are minute and sunk into the axis. Nat. size.

shaded area as when the paper was dinted, attracted the bees to the centre of the disc. Kugler (1943) finds it easier to train the bees to three-dimensional models than to completely flat coloured surfaces. The bees visited funnels up to 82 per cent more frequently than flat discs. Brian (1957) finds that bumble-bees react to the *inner* depth of the model, not to the outer. Honey-bees react to very small marks. Petals of *Hypericum perforatum*, marked with dots with a biro pen, were individually prodded by honey-bees with their tongues as part of their routine examination of the blooms which are, in fact, nectarless.

Appreciation of floral form is extended in the *Bombi* to that of the whole plant. Manning, (1956) has noticed that *Bombi* working the Hound's Tongue, *Cynoglossum officinale*, whose dull chocolate-coloured flowers do not form much contrast with the foliage, will approach plants from which all the flowers have been removed, and also plants of any other species which approximate to its pyramidal form, such as Ragwort, *Senecio jacobaea* and Figwort, *Scrophularia nodosa*. This perception of the plant form is used before that of the scent of the flower when foraging, for Hound's Tongue plants of a different shape, for example those in the rosette stage, although they had the correct scent, were not visited.

The degree to which the bumble-bees react to the form of the whole plant is modified by the "attractiveness" of the flower. Foxgloves in flower are not mistaken for Hound's Tongue although they are near to it in form. In this case the bees react to the colour and form of the flower alone, for foxglove plants with their flowers removed or in young bud, are ignored.

DISTANCE OF RECOGNITION OF FLOWERS

The sense of sight and not scent is employed by *Bombus* in distance recognition of flowers. Kugler (1943) proved this by the simple expedient of placing a glass cylinder, open at either end, over an inflorescence of *Stachys officinalis* (Betony). The scent could issue at the top and the bottom of the cylinder, but the *Bombi* flew straight to the sides of the glass through which they could see the flowers.

Crane (1957) finds that three tropical butterflies, *Heliconius erato*, *H. melpomenes* and *H. ricini*, which are primarily flower visitors, also use their sense of sight instead of their sense of smell when searching for food. They ignored *Lantana comosa* flowers which were concealed among foliage, although these were strongly scented. If even a single flower of the truss was exposed to view, the butterflies flew straight towards it.

The honey-bee probably reacts in the first instance to the scent rather than to the shape or colour of the flowers, for this is the one piece of specific information about the nature of the crop it receives from the dancing bee.

DEVELOPMENT OF THE PATTERN OF FORAGING BEHAVIOUR

Once the bee has visited the flower it will be in possession of many more facts. It will know the location of the crop and the colour, form and position of the flowers on the plant. It will also learn whether nectar or pollen is available. Through the contact of its feet, legs, head, belly and back with the flower parts, it will learn how the flower is orientated. Its tongue will learn the situation of the nectar, and its eyes will supplement their knowledge of the flower form with more intimate details such as the visual nectar guides. These may be reinforced by scent guides on the petals which the antennae may appreciate.

Hereafter the bee will react not to the flower scent alone, but to a pattern composed in some measure of all these floral attributes which it is able to perceive. The pieces of the pattern may not be the same for all foragers, but will depend on the individual bee's experience at the flower. For example, the flower may have been previously exploited for its pollen while the nectar is left untouched; this may lead to the bee foraging for nectar alone. The pattern may change as the foraging proceeds and the bee may cease to be stimulated by the attributes of the flower which originally attracted it.

The initial experience at a flower has a powerful influence on the subsequent behaviour of the forager. The first approach to a bloom is usually to the flower face, the legitimate floral approach. Should the insect succeed straightway in finding food, the next flower it visits will also be exploited legitimately. Failure to obtain recompense sometimes leads to illegitimate exploitation and reduces the pollination potential of the species. Should a short-tongued bumble-bee such as *Bombus terrestris* fail to reach the nectar of a long-tubed flower, say that of Red Clover, *Trifolium pratense*, it will examine the whole bloom, both inside and out, and finally bite through the corolla tube to obtain the nectar. Should it pierce the right-hand side of the tube and successfully thieve the nectar, it is likely to bite the next flower it visits at exactly the same spot. If a honey-bee, which often plays the role of a secondary thief on Red Clover, visits a flower punctured on the right-hand side, it will fly to the right side of the next flower in search of a similar backdoor entrance.

Brian (1957) reports that even thieving may be favourable to pollination. *Bombus lucorum* and *B. agrorum* workers thieve the nectar of *Lotus uliginosus* through the small gap left between the wings and standard at either side of the corolla. Again, first impressions are lasting: if a bee probes the right-hand gap first, it will subsequently always go to the right of a flower, and vice versa. These bees stole nectar, but also collected pollen by which they trip the flower in the usual way and pollinate it. This combination of thieving and legitimate working was actually to the advantage of the plant, for the bees worked more rapidly and visited more flowers per minute than those which only worked the flowers legitimately.

Brian (1957) finds that bumble-bees differ in behaviour and that this affects their choice of flowers. *Bombus lucorum* and *B. pratorum* are agressive in defence of their nests, and also towards other species in the field, where they tend to displace the gentler *B. agrorum*, driving it to visit deeper flowers than it would otherwise choose. They also tend to bite into the flower and rob it, if the nectar is not easily available. Such behaviour seldom benefits the plant, and Brian suggests that the evolution of long-tubed flowers was fostered by the long-tongued bees, such as *B. hortorum* which appears psychologically incapable of robbing them.

Bees are very quick to take advantage of any means to obtain their food. Sometimes quite fortuitous happenings will permit them to exploit and pollinate a flower they usually ignore. Such a one has been observed in *Convolvulus minor*. The trumpet-like corolla is very slippery and honey-bees seem unwilling to plunge into it and virtually stand on their heads to work it. On hot sunny days there was a partial wilting of the petals; in some flowers they flagged backwards, reducing the distance to the nectar and offering a better foothold. The bees discovered this and worked these flowers.

Honey-bees collect pollen in a way which is often highly individual. They differ in the speed and neatness with which they pack a load and also in the technique they employ. Two different ways of collecting were seen on the broom, *Sarothamnus scoparius* and on *Phacelia tanacetifolia*.

On the former, the method adopted by the majority is that described by Knuth (1905). The bee alights on a well-opened, but unsprung flower, extrudes its tongue and explores the base of the standard for the non-existent nectar. This pushing movement dislocates the keel petal, and the short stamens push up, striking the belly of the bee, while the long ones push up under the wing roots. The style delivers some of the pollen on to the back of the thorax. A goodly spray of pollen is borne away on the wind as the flower is sprung. The bee turns its attention to collecting such pollen as is left on the anthers. The short stamens are cleaned first, then the bee climbs the style and cleans it. One bee attained a high degree of efficiency in her mode of collecting the pollen. It ignored the open flowers and confined its visits to buds whose standard petal was raised but 2 mm above the wings. It pushed under the left-hand side of the standard, then, turning round and shouldering up the standard with its body, it proceeded down the keel, catching the stamens as they protruded in succession from the keel with its forelegs, and cleaning them of their pollen. Not a scrap of pollen was wasted. After its visits the flowers virtually closed again: it never dislocated the keel, although the anthers and tip of the style remained protruding from it as evidence of the complete exploitation of the pollen. This latter method of working *increased the potentiality for cross-pollination*. The flowers would receive a second visit from another worker, as they tend to seek out flowers which are unsprung.

Two methods of collecting pollen were seen on *Phacelia tanacetifolia*. The five anthers stand erect on thin, stiff filaments about 1 cm above the open corolla. The anther-lobes recurve strongly after their longitudinal dehiscence, and a small ball of violet pollen is presented. Some bees clung to the corolla and exploited the anthers by reaching up to them with their forelegs. The prettier technique resembled that of a helicopter. The bee hovers above the flower and neatly removes the pollen from the anthers with the first two pairs of legs. Then it backs off a little and packs to the hindlegs, then advances again for more pollen. Occasionally it alights on the corolla, takes a sip of nectar to cement its load, and returns to its hoverings, an unusual technique for a honey-bee. The plant sets abundant seed, a tribute to the efficiency of the bee as a pollinator.

The size of the pollen pellets gathered by the bees is remarkable: bumble-bees will carry up to 30 per cent of their weight in pollen. A honey-bee's load of Bluebell pollen (*Endymion nonscriptus*) weighed 22·8 mg. Each flower produces approximately 1·59 mg of pollen, so it had exploited at least 14 flowers. As the pollen is liberated gradually over a period of 4–76 hr, the number of flowers visited was far in excess of this figure. One forager with a huge load had shifted its centre of gravity so much that it fell over backwards. A similar mishap overtook a bee working *Aubrieta deltoidea*. Both, on picking themselves up, immediately made the circling orientation flight and returned to the hive.

PATTERNS OF FORAGING

The bumble- and honey-bees differ in their pattern of flight when foraging. Manning (1957) has observed two patterns in the former. He set out sixteen flower models in a square pattern of four rows of four and found the bees foraged in straight lines **orthogonally**, or in a square pattern and very seldom flew diagonally between the models. They adhere to this pattern in the field. They also conduct questing flights in wide sweeps when searching for new individuals of the crop they are foraging.

The honey-bee arriving at a crop, works the first plant she alights upon and then the neighbouring ones of the same species and tends to restrict her field to a few square yards. On subsequent visits she will nearly always return to the plant she first visited, and work around it again (Butler, 1945). This behaviour may have repercussions for the breeding potentialities of the flowers. It may break up any large stand of individuals into more or less isolated cross pollinated populations. Especially will this be so if the field-force of foragers is relatively small in numbers compared with the area of forage available.

Free (1962) also brings proof of the circumscription of foraging area, finding that honey-bees working Apple, Apricot,

Pear, Peach, Plum and Sweet Cherry, visit at most two trees during one foraging period, and that they only transfer pollen from one tree to the first few flowers they visit of the other.

Menke (1951) observed differences in the foraging behaviour of insects in Apple orchards. Whereas the honey-bees visited flowers on all parts of the trees, the Queen bumble-bees foraged chiefly in the top third of the tree and the Anthophorid bees in the top half. The Andrenas mostly confined their working to the sunny side of the tree and only worked during the hottest part of the day. The honey-, bumble- and Anthophorid-bees all worked intensively and also flew from tree to tree, but the Andrenas were only found on the fringe of the orchard bordering on waste land where they have their breeding ground. All these insects are valuable pollinators, but their concerted efforts would lead to more pollination in the tree tops than in the branches, unless the honey-bees were very numerous.

PATTERN OF FORAGING ON INDIVIDUAL PLANTS

A positive correlation occurs between the method of working employed by the insect visitor and the arrangement of the flowers on the plant. Manning has observed that the bumble-bees work from the bottom to the top of a racemose inflorescence such as that of Foxglove, *Digitalis purpurea*. The flowers are markedly protandrous. This, then, is a happy trait, ensuring cross-pollination of the older basal flowers which are in the female stage. If the bees worked from the tip of the inflorescence downwards, they would be more likely to effect self-pollination.

Schremmer (1960) states that *Xylocopa violacea* follows the same routine when working *Acanthus mollis* which has the same order of ripening of anthers and stigmas. This way of working the flowers is even more necessary here, for the valves of the stigma only open a week after anther dehiscence.

THE SIGNIFICANCE OF PHENOLOGY IN THE INSECT–FLOWER RELATIONSHIP

Phenological studies show intimate links exist between insects and flowers. The time of emergence of the adult insect, and its active periods, often coincides with the flowering of certain species. The vernal Andrenas, a genus of solitary bees, appear when the willows (*Salix* spp.) are in flower and chiefly confine their visits to them for both nectar and pollen. The autumnal Andrenas in North America have a similar bond with the golden-rods (*Solidago* spp.). *Halictus nelumbonis* visits only *Nymphaea advena* and a few other species of waterlily. Bees, which behave in this way, selecting but a few related host plants are said to be **oligotropic**. They usually fly for a limited period only during the year, appearing and disappearing with their particular flowers.

The oligotropic hibiscus bee, *Emphor bombiformis*, which gathers nectar and pollen almost exclusively from *Hibiscus lasiocarpus*, is at some pains to ensure continuance of its relationship with the plant. In some seasons the earth banks in which it nests are impenetrable through drought. In such a case the female transports water to moisten the soil sufficiently to enable her to excavate her burrow and provision it, so that the next generation arrives at the correct time in the following season, that is, when the hibiscus blooms again. The phenological correlation is remarkable, the plant blooming from July 20th to Sept. 16th, the male bee flying from July 21st to Sept 2nd, and the females from July 30th to Sept. 11th (Robertson, 1925).

Even closer associations occur: a classic example is that of a small solitary bee, *Halictoides novae-angliae* and the Pickerel-weed, *Pontederia cordata*. The flowering of the latter coincides with the appearance of the imago of the former and it is believed that this bee does not visit any other plant for nectar or pollen. It is therefore a **monotropic** bee. This constant association is remarkable, for many other flowers, with equally available food-stuffs, are in bloom at the same time, and *Pontederia* has other insect visitors besides *Halictoides*. Similar examples occur among the Lepidoptera. The moth *Micropteryx calthella* visits only buttercups and is therefore oligotropic or may even be monotropic. Crane (1957) states that tropical butterflies which visit flowers for nectar, as distinct from those which feed on fruit juices, tend to be oligotropic.

A curiously tenuous phenological relationship exists between the Mirror Ophrys (*O. speculum*) and its pollinator *Colpa aurea*, depending on the slight protandry of this species of wasp (*see* Pollination by Wasps).

The honey-bee, which is active at all seasons, will visit any flower from which it can obtain food: it is **polytropic**.

Bees which visit certain flowers for *pollen only*, fall into similar categories as those mentioned above and are termed **mono-**, **oligo-** and **polylectic** according to whether they confine their visits respectively to one or a few species of the same genus or are catholic in their tastes. These bees usually visit quite different flowers for nectar. According to Linsley (1956), among the solitary bees, the *Anthophorinae* are polylectic, and the *Eucerinae* oligolectic. In parts of Central and North America, two genera of the latter group, *Xenoglossa* and *Peponapis*, are very important pollinators of wild and cultivated Cucurbitas. They confine their pollen visits to this genus but visit a large number of other flowers for *nectar*.

Another phenological bond exists between flower and insect. The daily period of activity of the insect coincides with the time at which the flowers are open. There are two chief classes of anthophilous insects, diurnal and nocturnal, and also a few matutinal and crepuscular species. These are matched by day and night flowers. The diurnal insects are the social and solitary bees, the flies, and the butterflies. Some solitary bees, *Onagrandrena* spp. are matutinal, flying even before it is light. Linsley (1956) has observed that they buzz loudly while they are flying until the dawn breaks and then fly more quietly.

Moths are abroad in the dusk, when most night flowers are opening, and also during the night. More information is needed as to their actual period of flower visiting. *Plusia gamma*, the Silver Y moth is exceptional: it flies during the day and is commonly seen working Michaelmas daisies (*Aster* spp.) and *Nepeta* × *Faasenii* in autumn.

Linsley (1955) reports exquisitely precise phenological associations between flower and insect on the fringe of the Mojave desert in California, where three species of *Melandrena* bees all collect pollen exclusively from a single species, *Oenothera dentata* v. *johnsonii*. Each day, the time available for pollen collection is short, as the sun rapidly becomes too hot for the bees to work. In $1\frac{1}{4}$ hr, that is from 40 min *before dawn*, until 35 min after the sun reaches the flowers, they complete their foraging. The flowers seem to present their pollen at least in part before dawn, for the bees begin to collect it before it is light. Even within this brief period, there is a stratification of the foragers. *Melandrena mojavensis*, the largest bee, starts collecting first; *M. deserticola*, the smallest of the three is second, and *M. oenotherae*, which is intermediate in size between those two, is last in the field. Monolecty, under these peculiar desert conditions, virtually prohibits interspecific crossing, but ensures free gene exchange between the biotypes. Linsley and MacSwain (1956) have proposed a new subgenus *Onagrandrena* for these *Oenothera* bees and other allied species in view of their constant association with members of the Onagraceae.

CHAPTER IX

THE FEATURES OF ENTOMOPHILOUS FLOWERS

INSECT-POLLINATED flowers possess all the positive attributes of size, colour, scent and form which those pollinated by the natural agencies of wind and water lack. They have a conspicuous perianth composed of petals, but sepals or even a brush of stamens may replace them and impart a flower-like form, as in the Bottle-brush (*Callistemon*). The petals are coloured and scented and arranged to give various patterns, and these colours, scents and patterns are known to be those which anthophilous insects can *see*, *recognize* and *remember*.

But these features are all of secondary importance in their biology, the essential attribute is the presence of *insect food* within the flower, in the form of nectar, pollen or juicy tissues (see Chapters IV and V).

NECTAR AND POLLEN FLOWERS

Flowers may be divided into two main classes depending on the kind of food they offer to the visitor. The majority contain both nectar and pollen and we may call these the **nectar** flowers. Among these are the Red and White Clover, *Trifolium pratense*, and *T. repens*, Raspberry, *Rubus idaeus*; Blackberry, *R. fruticosus*; White Sweet Clover, *Melilotus alba*; Alfalfa, Apple, Peach, Cabbage, and Gum trees, *Eucalyptus*.

Others are nectarless but produce abundant pollen and are

called the **pollen** flowers. Such are the Poppies, Rock Rose, St. John's Wort, and Dog Rose. There are also the unisexual flowers of monoecious or dioecious plants, such as the Holly, the willows, and cucurbitas, where the male flowers have both nectar and pollen and the female flowers have nectar only.

TYPES OF POLLINATION

The second main division of **nectar** flowers is into those with potentialities for **promiscuous pollination**, and those with **non-promiscuous** or **restricted pollination**. This depends on the position of the nectar in the flower. If the nectar is freely exposed and virtually any insect short- or long-tongued can reach it, promiscuous pollination is possible. If the nectar is at the bottom of a corolla tube, and may only be exploited by certain long-tongued insects, pollination is non-promiscuous and limits are imposed on the potentiality for pollination.

Many positive relationships exist between insect structure and flower structure. That they are positive is in itself highly significant of their interdependence, indeed we cannot visualize the one group without the other. They may be demonstrated between the tongue length of the insect and the depth at which nectar is situated in the flower, between the colour vision of insects and flower colour, between flower form and insect shape, between the strength of the insect and the texture of the petals. Relationships also exist between the phenological rhythms of both insect and plant and even between the geographical distribution of plant and animal. So striking are these relationships that particular flowers are designated "bee", "bumble-bee", "moth", "butterfly", and "fly" flowers in respect of their form and their constant insect visitors.

Before delineating the characters of these groups separately, certain features, common to several of them, may be considered. These are flower scent; nectar guides and scent guides on the petals; and tongue guides within the corolla.

NECTAR GUIDES

Nectar guides are present on the petals of many insect-pollinated flowers. They take the form of blotches, streaks, or spots, either darker in colour than the rest of the petal, or of a different and contrasting colour. *Oxalis acetosella* has deep pink veins running longitudinally down the white or pink petals, *Veronica gentianoides* (Fig. 58) dark blue veins on pale blue and *Geranium versicolor* violet veins on lilac petals. *Rhododendron ponticum* has a pattern of brownish flecks on the light purple

Fig. 58. *Veronica gentianoides*, Scrophulariaceae, showing nectar guides in the form of dark blue stripes on the light blue petals. The widely diverging stamen filaments are grasped by the insect and bow, bringing the anthers in contact with its abdomen. ×4·5.

petals, Foxglove has deep purple spots ringed with white on the lower side of the bell and *Pontederia cordata* two bright yellow spots on the middle lobe of the upper lip.

Many Pelargoniums are blotched deep red or almost black at the base of the two upper petals which lie nearest to the nectary. Darwin observed that peloric or regular flowers of *Pelargonium* had no nectaries and that nectar guides were also absent. In a flower where the nectary was partly aborted only one of the upper petals bore a guide.

The young flowers of Horse Chestnut (*Aesculus hippocastanum*) (Fig. 3) have a yellow blotch on each of the two lower petals which changes first to orange and then to pink as the flower ages. Forget-me-not has a yellow coronal ring on the blue petals which fades to white with age and in *Borago officinalis* the central cone of purple-black anthers contrasts with the sky blue corolla. In *Narcissus poeticus* there is a brilliant orange "pheasant's eye" corona surrounded by white tepals, (Fig. 59).

FIG. 59. *Narcissus poeticus*, possesses both olfactory and visual nectar guides, the corona contrasting with the tepals in colour and scent. ×2·8.

Yellow-blue, white-blue, red-white, and yellow-white are all recognizable colour contrasts for the bee's eye. Dark streaks on a light background should also be discerned and probably truly act as guides too.

Daumer (1958) by photographing flowers through selective filters, has demonstrated the existence of colour patterns which are invisible to the human eye. The yellow tepals of *Iris pseudacorus*, which are concolorous to us, reflect ultraviolet strongly just around the entrance to the tube. This will be discernible by bees whose colour vision extends far into this range.

Flower scents are volatile essential oils and these themselves are complex mixtures of compounds. The constituents belong to many different groups of chemicals. The scent of rose is due to the aliphatic terpene alcohols geraniol, nerol and citronellol, and also to phenylethyl alcohol. Piperonal, an aromatic aldehyde, has the heliotrope odour which is found not only in the scent of *Heliotropium peruvianum* (Cherry Pie), but also, to a lesser degree, in that of *Filipendula ulmaria* (Meadow Sweet) and *Robinia pseudacacia* (False Acacia or Black Locust). α-Terpineol has a typical lilac odour and there is coumarin in the scent of *Galium odoratum* (Sweet Woodruff) and *Melilotus spp.* (Melilot or Sweet Clover). Several ketones have been isolated from natural scents which have a minty or violet odour, including parmone. α- and β-ionones also smell strongly of violet, the latter is found in the scent of *Boronia megastigma*. The scent of carnations is due to the phenols eugenol, methyleugenol and isoeugenol.

Little is known of the ecology of scent production by flowers. Diurnal species emit scent during the day, while nocturnal flowers are scented chiefly, or only, at night, even though the flowers may remain open during the day as in the Honeysuckle, *Lonicera periclymenum*.

The scents of nocturnal flowers differ in kind from those of day flowers being very "sweet" and not "spicy", except for the bat flowers, which smell mousy and sour. Some orchids are said to have different day and night scents (Hampton, 1925). *Dendrobium glumaceum* has a heliotrope scent in the morning and is lilac-scented at night. *Phalaenopsis schilleriana* changes from lily-of-the-valley scent during the day to rose scent at night.

The petals of *Pelargonium*, all the Labiate flowers and nearly all the Scrophulariaceae are *scentless*: the foliage is fragrant in the first two families. There is some association between flower colour and scent: white flowers have a higher percentage of scented blooms than any other colour. *Pure* blue Gentians, Delphiniums and Aquilegias and also pure scarlet flowers are seldom scented.

SCENT GUIDES

Lex (1954), in a series of ingenious experiments has shown that scent guides are present on flower petals. She separated the white perianth and orange corona of *Narcissus poeticus* (Fig. 59) and enclosed them in different dishes which she gave to humans to sniff, taking the precaution of covering the petals with net to obviate subjective factors. Humans judged the two parts to smell differently. She then trained bees to visit the perianth by placing a feeding dish of sugar syrup (scentless) above the container. Then she removed the syrup and altered the position of the perianth container and also offered one with the coronas. The bees sought out the perianth alone, showing that they too distinguished between two scents. The reverse experiment was equally successful. Thus the central corona is shown to have a different scent from that of the perianth, and as the bees can distinguish this it may act as a scent guide to the nectar.

Another interesting case is that of the Horse Chestnut (*Aesculus hippocastanum*). The young flowers bear a yellow spot on their lower petals. In older flowers it changes to pinky red (Fig. 3). Lex shows that the *colour* change is accompanied by a *change in the scent* which the bees perceived, so they are able to distinguish between the young and older flowers. Here we have both an optical and an olfactory change to aid the insect.

TONGUE GUIDES

Quite apart from the provision of nectar guides on the petals, tongue guides are present in many flowers and, as they are a *positive* feature of flower structure, no doubt have some significance in the animal–flower relationship.

When one begins to exploit flowers for nectar with a capillary pipette, it soon becomes evident that the *direction* of the probing is guided by the shape of the *interior* of the flower into the correct channel leading to the nectar. This is not simply that the probe reaches the bottom of the corolla tube, but finds that portion of it in which the nectar collects. This guidance may start, for the insect, before the mouth of the tube is entered, by the provision of bumps, knobs or hairs on the landing platform.

163

The four parallel fringes on the labellum of *Ceologyne cristata*; the uncompromisingly stiff, inwardly directed hairs on the lower lip of *Rhinanthus minor*; the lateral knobs on the lower lip of the corolla of *Galeopsis segetum* or *G. speciosa* (Schremmer, 1953) are accredited examples. Yet another is seen in the flower of *Paulownia tomentosa*, the Foxglove Tree (Fig. 60) which has a deep central channel running down the lower lip into the corolla tube, and also has two lateral grooves. All lead to the nectary, which surrounds, and is fused, to the base of the ovary. The two pairs of anthers are tilted slightly outwards to face the lateral grooves, while the bent swollen tip of the style, with its flat buttonlike stigma, lies opposite the centre channel. The nectar collects chiefly in the lower side of the tube, opposite the central tongue guide.

Insects differ in their ability to place their tongue accurately in a narrow tube, and even a very small corolla, i.e. the expanse of the terminal lobes as distinct from the tube, may, in itself, be a valuable aid as a tongue guide. Petal lobes and the top part of the corolla tube were removed from the flowers of *Buddleia variabilis* and *Kentranthus ruber* and a big *Bombus* queen, stabbing at the tubes with its long tongue, only succeeded in reaching its goal about once in four to five attempts. On the other hand, the honey-bees, which were exploiting a source usually inaccessible to them, probed accurately every time.

The internal guides are fashioned in various ways. The corolla and stamens and style may all contribute and many examples of this collaboration are found among the Crucifers. In *Arabis albida* the four long stamens and style block the centre of the flower, dividing the corolla in two and leaving a narrow channel between themselves and the short stamen, so that the insect's tongue is guided only to the base of the latter where the nectar drop is situated.

In *Freesia refracta*, *Streptocarpus rexii* and *Strobilanthus isophylla*, and some trumpet daffodils, the guide is a function of the filaments of the epipetalous stamens. In *Freesia refracta*, the three filaments and style all come to lie at the lower side of the corolla and block this part of the tube. The downward deflection of the posterior filament neatly divides the corolla

FIG. 60a. *Paulownia tomentosa*, Scrophulariaceae. Corolla with deep central channel forming a tongue guide. × 1·4.

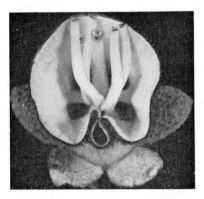

FIG. 60b. *Paulownia tomentosa*, Scrophulariaceae. Section towards base showing guide leading to site of nectar at lower side of corolla. × 3·3.

tube into two halves, each of which becomes a separate chamber at the point where the filament becomes epipetalous. The insect's tongue is guided firstly along and between the smooth runnels formed by the style and lower filaments, and then left or right towards the base of the corolla tube.

Aestivation may be responsible for the formation of the flower tube. This is prettily seen in *Reinwardtia trigyna* (Linaceae). Although the flower is polypetalous, a tube is formed by the strong contortion of the clawed petals. This contortion is preserved by a minute tongue on the claw which points upwards, and also by the channelled edges of the petals which dovetail into one another. Each claw has a median ridge and these latter, together, divide the tube into five channels or internal tongue guides. The centre of the tube is blocked by the erect anthers and filaments and the three styles. The anthers dehisce sideways, so that the pollen is presented on the inner side of the tongue guide channel.

FALSE TONGUE GUIDES

Abutilon megapotamicum (Fig. 61) has a pendant flower, the pillar-box red gamosepalous calyx contrasting with the narrow tube of contorted yellow petals. Both nectar and tongue guides are present. The nectar guides are unevenly distributed on the inner face of the petals, there are four strong claret-coloured streaks on one side and three or four faint streaks on the other. The side of the petal which is overlapped by its neighbour in the contortion bears the faint streaks. Each set of streaks unites into one streak towards the base of the petal and flank its curved *tubular* base. This, then, is the remarkable feature: the tongue is led straight into one of these five petal tubes which are completely dry. A narrow lenticular space exists between the petals which is only half the width of the tubed base, this leads to the abundant nectar in the *sepal* cup. Blind probing results in a few lucky hits. The nectar is so plentiful that it runs up the outside of the petals, even to the level of the mouth of the calyx, but the inside of the flower remains dry. Honey-bees and hover flies then exploit it by thrusting their tongues between the tips of the sepals.

A similar state of affairs occurs in *Billbergia nutans*. Scales between the filaments of the stamens appear tubed like a hellebore petal. They are actually only strongly curved, but their edges abut on the corolla lobes whose median vein sticks out and assists in sealing the "tube". Five chambers are thus formed which act as false tongue guides, as the nectar is secreted by the

Fig. 61. *Abutilon megapotamicum*, Malvaceae. Bird-Flower. Nectar is secreted at the base of the flask-shaped calyx. × 1·7.

top of the ovary which is below their insertion. There is virtually no access to this, because the style occupies the centre of the flower tube, and the filaments of the stamens fill in the gaps between the scales. The tongue is led into the dry interior of the flower, while the nectar wells up and slides along the outside of the scales; so the latter are not acting as tongue guides, except, falsely. But they do narrow the tube of the flower so that the nectar rises to a height at least equal to the level of the tips of the scales, that is 9 mm above the ovary (Fig. 62).

One may note that both these species with false tongue guides are not insect but bird pollinated.

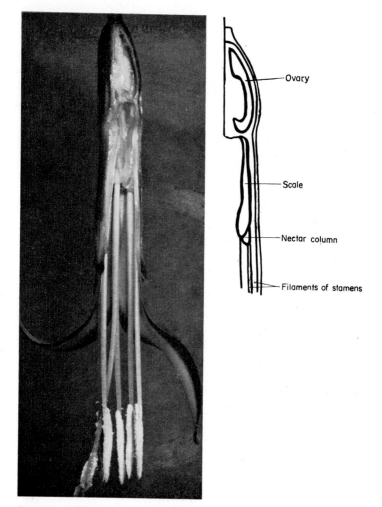

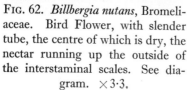

FIG. 62. *Billbergia nutans*, Bromeliaceae. Bird Flower, with slender tube, the centre of which is dry, the nectar running up the outside of the interstaminal scales. See diagram. ×3·3.

BEE FLOWERS

Bees are the chief flower visitors; collectively they visit more flowers than all the other groups of anthophilous insects. Firstly, it is necessary to distinguish between the flowers visited solely for their pollen and those visited for nectar and pollen. The former may belong to almost any flower class, the latter, too, are varied in size and shape, but in all of them the nectar is in some degree protected, and they are usually incapable of being promiscuously pollinated.

The primary relation is between the length of the corolla tube and the tongue length of the bee.

RHYTHM

Bee flowers are chasmogamic and open during the day, but within this period species have their own rhythms. For example, the poppies (pollen flowers) bloom between 5 and 6 a.m. and have often completed their life by midday, while virtually all the new buds of the Broad Bean, *Vicia faba* open first in the afternoon, 74 per cent of them between noon and 2 p.m. Many composite inflorescences have a definite opening and closing rhythm. Dandelions open within $\frac{1}{2}$ hr of the sun striking them, begin to close 3 hr later, and are shut within 5 hr on a normal sunny day. They do not open during rain and only open slowly if it is dull. This behaviour is nicely geared to that of the bees which are stimulated to forage chiefly by a high light intensity.

COLOUR

All known flower colours occur amongst bee flowers. Blues, purple, reddish purple, yellows and oranges are common and these are all within the range of the colour vision of the bees. The colours are moreover strongly saturated being much brighter and deeper than the pale shades of moth flowers. Pure red is rare except in poppies. These together with many white and yellow flowers reflect ultraviolet strongly. This is the most attractive "colour" to bees.

FORM

The medium- and long-tongued bee flowers are found chiefly among the climax groups of the Angiosperms, particularly the

Papilionaceae, the Personales, the Lamiales, and the Compositae. These flowers, with the exception of the legumes, are all sympetalous and those of the first three groups are markedly zygomorphic.

The Labiate has a two-lipped corolla (Figs. 5 and 50). The lower lip is variously fashioned to form a platform on which the bee alights. The stamens and style in the North temperate region species stand erect and somewhat overarch the platform. They are usually under the shelter of the upper lip of the corolla. This kind of flower is admirably suited to both the hive- and bumble-bee. When probing for nectar, they receive the pollen on their backs, from whence they clear it with their leg combs and transfer it to their torsal pollen baskets. Flowers shedding their pollen on to the insect's back are termed **nototribic**.

In **sternotribic** flowers such as the composites (Fig. 20), legumes (Fig. 51), and *Pycnostachys urticifolia* (Fig. 53), the positions are reversed. The stamens and style are housed in the somewhat keel-shaped lower lobe and the upper lobe is small. This arrangement is particularly suited to bees with abdominal brushes such as the Leaf-cutter, *Megachile* and other Dasygastrae, who collect their pollen by direct contact with the anthers.

We cannot say that this is an adaptation to bees of this type, for many bees with tarsal brushes collect pollen from sternotribic flowers, for example, honey-bees work clovers. Contrarily, many with abdominal brushes collect from nototribic flowers, tackling them by turning around after landing so that their brushes contact the anthers, e.g. as does *Megachile circumcincta* K. on Salvias (Schremmer, 1953). Nevertheless, Robertson (1923) has found that some of the sternotribic Papilionaceae in America are virtually dependent for pollination on the Dasygastrae as those bees are almost the only insects which visit them. This suggests that the flowers have been adapted to the bees.

In the Labiates there is no hindrance to probing the tubes, the corolla mouth is *open*, but there is a stratification of visitors depending on the *length* of the tube. The limit for the hive bees is about 7 mm. The tongue is 6 mm long, but the nectar often rises high enough in the tube for them to work somewhat deeper flowers. One must remember that if the tongue is able to touch the meniscus *all* the nectar can be removed. In the British flora, the small-flowered mints and thymes, and also Lavender, Rosemary and *Nepeta* × *faassenii*, the familiar grey-leaved edging-plant with lilac flowers, are all favourite honey-bee flowers. The Dead Nettles, white, red, and yellow, with corolla tubes 10–20 mm, *Galeopsis*, the Hemp Nettle (13–34 mm); the Ground Ivy, *Glechoma hederacea* (15–20 mm) and the Sages, *Salvia* (10–25 mm) are bumble-bee flowers.

The Salvias have a specialized "turnpike" floral mechanism. There are only two stamens. Each is joined shortly to the side of the corolla by its filament. Only half the anther is fertile, the sterile half being transformed into a flat strap of tissue. The two fertile halves are carried up on elongated stalks of connective tissue to the shelter of the upper lip of the corolla. The two sterile straps join together and form a plate, which, suspended as it is in the mouth of the petal tube, partly blocks it (Fig. 63). The bee on entering pushes against the plate which yields to its touch and swings the anthers down onto its back.

The British Scrophulariaceae are chiefly bee flowers but they have several features which exclude the hive-bee. The foremost of these is the **personate** corolla such as we see in the Snapdragon, *Antirrhinum majus* and the toadflax, *Linaria vulgaris.* The pouched lower lip is thrust up strongly against the bulging upper lip, completely closing the mouth of the flower. Considerable strength is needed to press it down, and moreover the landing platform is oblique and slippery. The powerful bumble-bees have no difficulty in exploiting the flowers: the honey-bee only manages to gain entrance after a hard struggle.

NECTAR SPURS

Another feature of bumble-bee flowers is that of nectar deep-seated in spurred petals. *Linaria* among the Scrophulariaceae, and *Delphinium, Aquilegia* and *Aconitum* among the Ranunculaceae, *Fumaria* and *Viola* all have long spurs. The petals are all fashioned in the same way, having a lobe at the top and then narrowing into a tube which has nectar-secreting tissue at the end. *Viola* differs in that the spur does not secrete but only acts as a reservoir for the nectar oozing from the two long tongue-like nectaries on the filaments of the two front stamens.

The pansies just come within the range of the honey-bee's tongue, but it often tackles the flower "upside down", alighting

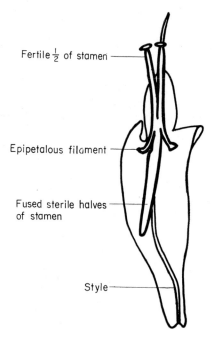

Fertile ½ of stamen

Epipetalous filament

Fused sterile halves of stamen

Style

Fig. 63. Diagram.

on the top petals and bending over to probe so that its back is turned towards the ground. Bumble-bees work the flowers normally, that is they fly directly to the face of the flowers. *Viola odorata* is exploited rapidly and easily by *Anthophora pilipes*, a large black solitary bee, which has an exceptionally long tongue of 21 mm.

In *Tropaeolum majus*, another favourite bumble-bee flower, the posterior sepal is spurred and nectar-secreting. The anthers are erected one by one before it in the direct path of the visitor.

There are some bumble-bee flowers in which the size of the corolla and its inner shape approximate to the size and shape of the insect as in the Turtlecap, *Chelone glabra*, and species of

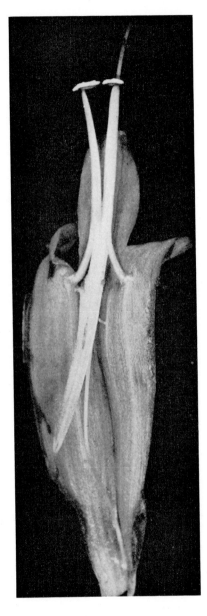

FIG. 63. *Salvia* sp. Corolla tube slit and opened out to show the plate, formed from the sterile halves of the anthers, which the bee, on entering, deflects backwards, swinging the fertile halves with the pollen down onto its back. See diagram. ×5.

173

Aconitum (Monkshood). Thus the hairy body always brushes against the stigmas and anthers, ensuring pollination.

The Foxglove, *Digitalis purpurea*, is also admirably proportioned for pollination by bumble-bees, being just wide enough at the top to hold the bee steady while it is drinking, and narrow enough at the mouth for it to brush the forked stigma and anthers as it enters. They zoom up into the flowers with great speed and accuracy, but the inclined bell completely defeats the efforts of the hive-bee to enter it. Occasionally they manage to cling to the filaments and collect pollen, but they cannot reach the nectar. The glove is too narrow for them to use their wings, and too wide for them to obtain purchase on the sides and "chimney" up. One was seen to crawl along the top of the corolla and reach over the lip. It succeeded in scratching out a little pollen from the foremost anthers, but then flew away and did not return to the flowers.

FLOWER PREFERENCES OF BEES

Inflorescences. Long-tubed flowers massed together into dense heads as for example in the Centaureas, are particularly attractive to long-tongued bees. Robertson (1923) found that 37·7 per cent of their visits were to this type of flower. After these massed short-tubed flowers were most favoured (22·1 per cent of visits). At first glance, it would appear that the former type was first favourite, but this may not be so. Up to the end of June the bees preferred the *long* flowers, after June the *shorter* ones. As these bees nearly all have a late seasonal maximum, it may be that their real preference is for the *shorter* flowers. An alternative explanation is that the late summer flora in this part of America (Illinois) has a preponderance of short-tubed flowers. However, Brian (1957) shows that *Bombus lucorum*, *B. agrorum* and *B. pratorum* undoubtedly prefer flowers considerably shorter than their tongues. Funnel-shaped paper flowers, 1 cm, 3 cm and 5 cm deep were offered to the bees and received 382, 238 and 143 visits respectively. Further evidence that this is a real preference comes from a second experiment. The bees were allowed to feed for one day at shallow flowers. Next day, given a choice of models, they visited 60 shallow, 25 medium and 5 deep "flowers". After a day's training on deep flowers, they visited 80 shallow, 40 medium and 25 deep "flowers" showing that they truly preferred the short-tubed ones.

Short-tongued bee flowers. Short-tongued bees strongly prefer short-tubed flowers massed into flat-headed inflorescences. Robertson (1923) found that 46·7 per cent of their visits were to this kind of flower. Next in order of preference were short-tubed flowers on separate pedicels (24·4 per cent). The former comprise chiefly the Asterae group of the Compositae and there are many of the Rosaceae, Cruciferae, short-flowered Labiates, Legumes and Veronicas among the latter.

CARPENTER-BEE FLOWERS

Pijl (1954) and Schremmer (1960) describe certain species as being specially adapted to pollination by the Carpenter bees (*Xylocopa*). These are very large and powerful insects, prone to thieve nectar from any flowers which have no protection for their corolla tubes. The *Xylocopa* flowers are so strongly made that even these bees are forced to exploit them legitimately. They belong to widely differing genera taxonomically but share certain features. They are large and have deep-seated nectar which is protected by the especially tough, coriaceous base of the corolla tube. In *Acanthus mollis* and *Thunbergia grandiflora* Roxb. the entrance to the nectar chamber is very narrow. It is a mere slit in the latter and in both it is further protected by a thick fringe of hairs. In *Thunbergia* the broad bases of the filaments interlock by means of ridges on their inner sides and completely occlude the chamber. They have to be forcibly parted before the insect is able to reach the nectar. Altogether a formidable barrier is erected against an illegitimate visitor, and only *Xylocopa latipes* is strong enough to gain entrance. Pijl considers *Thunbergia grandiflora* to be a "super-adapted" bee flower since it is entirely dependent on this one species of bee for satisfactory pollination. It is moreover, self-sterile.

Acanthus mollis (Fig. 30), has a broad landing-platform formed of the three lower petals. There is no upper lip to the corolla, its place being taken by a tough springy sepal which forms a hood over the platform. The floor of the platform arches up to meet the sepal and then, curving down, leads to the nectar chamber. The stamens have strongly bowed stout cartilaginous filaments which hold the anthers transversely above and parallel to the platform and just before the mouth of the tube. The anthers open by a longitudinal slit which faces downwards, but

Fig. 64. *Cassia corymbosa*, Papilionaceae. The flower has five short "fodder" stamens and two long "pollinating" stamens. *Xylocopa* vibrates its body to release pollen from the latter. ×2·25.

the pollen is held in place by thick fringes of hairs along their edges. *Xylocopa violacea* alights on the platform and thrusts forward into the flower, parting the anthers left and right and receiving some pollen on its sides. The anthers are so strongly held by their filaments that only a bee as powerful as the Carpenter can shoulder them apart. Some *Xylocopa* flowers have special "fodder" stamens with non-viable pollen for their visitors as well as "pollinating" stamens whose grains will germinate. In *Melastoma malabathricum* L. and related species, this double provision is matched by a twofold method of exploitation. The *Xylocopa* lands on the filaments of the fodder stamens and empties them first with its mouthparts. When this is complete, the bee, with wings at rest, vibrates its whole body and showers down the pollen from the fertile stamens onto its back. Much of it is trapped by the body hairs and will be transported to other flowers. The stigma too comes in contact with the bee's back during the visit (Pijl, 1954).

Species of *Cassia* also have fodder and pollinating stamens (Fig. 64) and the latter are "vibrated" as in *Melastoma*. In *Cassia bacillaris* L. both types of anthers have viable pollen.

FLY FLOWERS

According to Robertson (1924) flies, next to the bees, visit more species of flowers and make more flower visits than any other group of anthophilous insect; but their importance as pollinators is very much less. Those with thick probosci, such as the Muscoidea are more valuable than those with slender nectar-probing tongues, for pollen adheres more readily to them. The Syrphids (Hover Flies) which eat pollen, make a high percentage of non-pollinating visits, particularly to diclinous species for here they chiefly select the male flowers (68·2 per cent to male as against 31·7 per cent to female flowers). Willis and Burkhill (1895) compared the records of insect visitors to species growing both in Europe and in Britain. Far more short-tongued flies were seen on the British specimens and they concluded that these played a more important role in pollination here than on the continent.

The amount of pollination likely to be effected by flies also depends on the habitat. Moist sheltered positions are suitable habitats for myriads of species which cannot survive in windy or dry environments. The flowers growing in such areas will naturally receive a great many visits from flies, but such fortuitous associations have probably not led to any adaptive modification between insect and flower. Kugler (1939) found that sheltered plants of *Veronica chamaedrys* and *Circaea lutetiana* were pollinated by Syrphids but those in dry exposed places were pollinated by *Halictus* bees. In both these flowers the two stamens stand out on stiff filaments, one on either side of the corolla tube, and the style projects centrally (Fig. 58). The insect alights on the filaments and grasps them while probing for nectar. They bend with its weight and this brings the anthers together beneath the abdomen and dusts it with pollen, from whence it may be brushed off onto the stigma of another flower. The bees, being heavier, work this mechanism more efficiently.

SHORT-TONGUED FLY FLOWERS

Flowers visited by short-tongued flies are shallow, with accessible nectar and massed in flattish inflorescences. They include many Umbellifers such as Sea Holly, *Eryngium maritimum*, Parsnip, *Pastinaca sativa*, Hog-weed, *Heracleum sphondylium*. The Elder, *Sambucus nigra*, Rowan Tree, *Sorbus aucuparia*, and the short-tubed composites such as Yarrow, *Achillea millefolium* and the Golden-pods, *Solidago* spp. are very popular.

LONG-TONGUED FLY FLOWERS

The best known British plant is the primrose *Primula vulgaris*. The corolla tube is long and narrow and the top a salver-shaped landing-platform. The pollinators *Bombylius major* (Fig. 56), and other species of Bee-fly, with their long, permanently extended tongues, appear to exploit the flower while hovering before it like a Hawkmoth, but in fact they place either the first or last pair of legs on the petals. There is an ecological link between plant and insect, both of them are woodland species.

FLY TRAP FLOWERS

These are highly specialized and curiously formed flowers such as the Aristolochias (Fig. 10) and Ceropegias (Asclepiadaceae) or inflorescences like the Arums and Caladiums (Araceae). All have slippery-sided deep funnels leading to a chamber wherein the insects are imprisoned and where they come in contact with the stamens and ovaries. In the Aristolochias and Ceropegias the funnel may be lined with downward-pointing hairs, which prevent egress. In *Aristolochia clematitis* (Fig. 11), which is naturalized in parts of Britain, each hair is shaped like a seesaw but with one arm longer than the other (Fig. 12). The long arm points down the tube and is easily deflexed in that direction. The reverse movement is prevented by the short arm, which is only a very large protruding cell, coming into contact with the wall of the funnel. This is the principle of the fisherman's eel trap. The flowers are markedly protogynous the six-lobed stigma becoming receptive two to three days before anther dehiscence. It is visited by small midges of the Chironomidae, Mycetophilidae and Ceratopogonidae.

The spathe of *Arum nigrum* is a most delicately constructed fly trap (Knoll, 1926). The cells of the lower part of the mouth of the spathe, and also of the upper part of the chamber below have *oily* surfaces. Once a fly has slipped and fallen into the chamber, it cannot escape because its suction-pads are rendered useless by the oil. The conditions within the chamber are ideal for the delicate visitors (species of *Psychoda*). It is humid and is, moreover, *ventilated* by means of intercellular spaces connecting through the wall from the inner to the outer epidermis. The flies remain active until a day later, when the epidermis of the floral axis shrinks and wrinkles and they can obtain a purchase on it, and climb out, well dusted with pollen, to visit another spathe. This self-sterile plant sets abundant seed so this mechanism for cross-pollination is efficient.

Each female flower of *Arum maculatum* secretes a drop of nectar from its stigma (Fig. 28) and the "stigmas" of abortive flowers tend to block the entrance to the chamber.

SCENT

Fly flowers usually smell unpleasantly of sweat, faeces, urine or bad meat, that is, the smell is **aminoid**. It is the smell which is the *primary* distance attraction to the flower. This was proved by experiments with *Arum*. As the spathe opens, the spadix, which is full of starch, respires rapidly raising the temperature in the spathe by as much as 13°C. It was believed that this warmth attracted the insects. Glass models were made of the spathe and the false spadix was heated electrically. Some models were scented with the smell of the spadix, others were not. The flies were only attracted to the former, proving that the scent was the primary attraction.

COLOURS OF FLY FLOWERS

In open flat inflorescences yellow, white and greenish pre-dominate. The corollas of *Aristolochia, Stapelia, Caladium* and *Ceropegia* are commonly mottled, blotched or barred with brown, purple and dull red. Kugler (1956) found that newly emerged flies were not attracted by any colour. Colour, however, becomes meaningful if it is associated with scent, and, curiously enough, an innate preference seems to manifest itself, for when Carrion flies were offered artificial flowers of *different* colours but all possessing the same carrion smell, they spontaneously chose the dull purples and reds instead of yellow. Blue-bottles (*Calliphora*) and Green-bottles (*Lucilia*) have a well-developed colour sense and the latter react spontaneously to yellow and can distinguish it from blue.

OUTLINE OF FLOWERS

Some Aristolochias have long tails to the corolla and these too have been proved to be attractive to flies. Kugler (1956) offered *Sarcophaga* (Grey Flesh-flies) equal-sized model flowers, one fashioned as a cruciform disc, the other elliptical and with one end cut into seven long points. Both models were scented and had a hole leading to a phial of sugar near the centre. Sixty-one per cent of the flies' visits were to the latter, so they perceive and react positively to a shape which has tails.

SHINING SURFACES

Calliphora and other flies are attracted by any shining, liquid looking surface. The erumpent nectar disc of the Umbellifers and *Euonymus europaeus*, the Spindle Tree, has just this appearance, and so also have the sticky-looking yellow knobs of the staminodes of *Parnassia palustris*, although these latter do not secrete. They are said to inveigle unintelligent flies to explore them, but some quickly learn the true position of the nectar and exploit it without paying any attention to the stamin-odes. Nevertheless they may act as distance optical guides.

MOVING PARTS

Any vibrating or dangling appendage to a flower, particularly if it glistens, is said to attract flies. In *Ceropegia Haygarthii*, instead of the corolla having a "lantern" top to the tube as in *C. Woodii* (Fig. 65) it flares out to a trumpet shape, partitioned across the centre, and terminates in a slender stalk bearing a shining knob with fluttering hairs above its cavernous maw (Vogel, 1954).

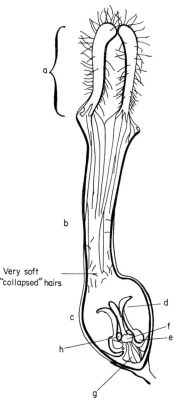

FIG. 65. *Ceropegia Woodii*. Fly-trap flower. a. Lobes of corolla forming a lantern, b. corolla tube with collapsed hairs, c. basal chamber, d. coronal appendage, e. nectar secreting base of appendage, f. style, g. the two carpels, h. part of an anther. ×5.

Very soft "collapsed" hairs

LIGHT WINDOWS

McCann (1943) describes an ingenious method of lighting the interior of fly flowers by means of "light windows" in the corolla. As he points out, flies trapped at the base of long tubes would tend to become inactive in the darkness. This is guarded against by the provision of translucent strips or patches of tissue which enable the light to penetrate, and which, by their

181

position, actually allow it to be directed so that it highlights the stamens. The swollen base of the *Ceropegia* flower has these "windows" either in the form of vertical strips or as a circular band near the top or base of the globe. *Cryptocoryne*, an aroid, has similar windows, but of a grille pattern, on the shoulder of the chamber of the spathe just opposite the cluster of male flowers, and the trapped flies, flying upwards to the light in a bid to escape, become dusted with pollen. Later they are liberated by the withering of a retaining valve in the latter inflorescence, and by the tilting of the flower and collapse of the hairs in its throat in the former case.

DO FLY FLOWERS EXIST?

Robertson (1924) states that no species of fly has a primary relation to flowers, but is phenologically associated with the insect it parasitizes and the food on which its larvae feed.

Kugler (1955) is of the opinion that positive adaptations of flies to plants and vice versa are rare, except between the sense of smell of Carrion flies and the carrion scent of flowers they visit. This is not always the case, for in South Africa, a remarkable group of long-tongued flies exists which visits flowers as highly modified to their needs as is any moth flower to a Sphingid. Indeed, the correspondence between them is of the same order of precision and delicacy.

The tongues are phenomenally long, 30–47 mm in species of *Pangonia* (Tabanidae) and that of the Nemestrid, *Megistorhynchus longirostris* reaches 60–70 mm. The tongue is hollow and suctorial and hangs down vertically, and the fly hovers in flight. All these features match those of the flowers they visit, for example *Lapeyrousia fabricii* (Iridaceae) has a narrow-tubed corolla 100 mm in length. It is flat-topped, has the anthers and styles positioned just above the mouth of the tube and the flower is carried erect on its pedicel.

MOTH FLOWERS

Most of the moth flowers are nocturnal. They open in the evening and the styles become receptive and the anthers dehisce also about this time. In the case of the tobaccos, *Nicotiana* spp.

and the Night-scented Stock, *Matthiola bicornis*, the petals regain their turgor which is lost when bright light impinges on them in the morning. The scent is also present at night; moreover the fragrances are different in kind from those of day flowers and strong and sweet to our senses. They are pale in colour, white, cream and light yellow shades predominate as in *Lychnis alba*, *Oenothera biennis*, *Lonicera periclymenum* and *Nicotiana affinis*. The flowers have very long tubes and the petal lobes stand at right angles to the ground. They present a flat face to the insect so that there is no lip or landing platform on which it may alight, as for example in *Gladiolus*, *Lonicera* and *Calystegia sylvestris*. This is finely adapted to the habit of flight of the moth, which hovers before the flower, while the tongue alone probes to the base of the corolla tube. The flowers may also be pendant as in the Daturas, or partly so as in some species of *Nicotiana*, and here too, are more easily exploited by a hovering insect. The texture of the petals is, generally speaking more delicate than that of bee- or bird-pollinated flowers.

Some diurnal flowers are associated with day-flying hawk-moths *Kentranthus ruber*, the Red Valerian, whose pollinator is the Humming-bird hawk-moth, *Macroglossa stellatorum* L. has the long tube which is characteristic of the group, but has "day" colours, red or pink, and a small landing platform and the flower is held almost erect, more after the manner of butterfly flowers.

Chamaenerion angustifolium, the Rose-bay Willow-herb, is interesting for its flowers seem to be partly adapted for day pollination by bees, and partly for night pollination by moths. The petals present a vertical face such as we see in moth flowers, and it is said that the nectar is produced in the evening; yet the stamens dehisce during the day, and the bright carmine of the petals is a "day" colour. The honey-bees visit them freely, collecting large loads of the bright blue pollen. Are they also attractive to moths?

There are also several day species, for example *Delphinium*, *Petunia*, *Rhododendron* and *Silene*, usually considered to be "bumble-bee" or "butterfly" flowers, which do not reclose after opening and are available for exploitation by crepuscular moths. Although they have day colours—blue, purple and deep carmine, they also have long tubes, and it is interesting to find that the Striped Hawkmoth, *Deilephila livornica* prefers this blue–violet–purple colour range. It will visit these flowers when it is almost dark instead of any yellow–green ones which are more visible to us, although it does also visit Tobacco and Honeysuckle.

LENGTH OF COROLLA TUBE AND TONGUE LENGTH

The length of the corolla tube ranges from 8–10 mm in *Kentranthus ruber* to nearly 30 cm in *Angraecum sesquipedale*, a Madagascan orchid. The tongues of the moths also vary greatly; some are prodigiously long. The Convolvulus Hawkmoth, *Herse convolvuli* (Fig. 54), has a tongue three times as long as its body, that is 87 mm. A South African species, *Coelonia fulvinotata* reaches 98 mm (Table 6). There is a remarkable parallelism between flower-tube length and tongue length; each flower has a moth whose tongue matches it. Indeed, Wallace correctly predicted that a Hawkmoth would be discovered whose tongue would be sufficiently long to exploit the spur of *Angraecum sesquipedale*.

TABLE 6. Tongue lengths of moths

Species	Common name	Country	Length of tongue in mm
Plusia gamma	Silver Y moth	European	15
Macroglossa stellatorum	Humming-bird Hawkmoth	British Isles	25–28
Herse convolvuli	Convolvulus Hawkmoth	Europe	65–80
Coelonia fulvinotata		South Africa	98
Macrosilia morgani praedicta		Madagascar	225
Cocythius cluentius		Brazil	250

Successful pollination of night flowers depends on the relation between the length of the corolla tube and the position of the anthers and stigmas on the one hand; and the tongue length and position of the insect's body on the other. If the insect's head, back or belly is brought into contact with the essential organs when probing, then the "fit" is satisfactory. This is the case when *Macroglossa stellatorum* exploits *Lonicera periclymenum*. Its legs are tucked up flat along the side of its body, and the stamens and style brush against the belly.

The level of the nectar in the flower tube is, however, pertinent and deducted from the tube length, may give a truer picture of the actual tongue length required. Table 7 gives data showing the height to which nectar may rise and so alter the distance that the insect has to probe.

TABLE 7. Length of flower tube and height of nectar in tube

Species	Type of pollinator	Length flower tube mm	Height of nectar in tube in mm
Coleus thrysoideus	bee	9·2	3·4
Nepeta × *faasenii*	bee	9·5	5
Citrus paradisi	bee	14	5
Echeveria retusa hybrida	bee	13	4·3
Digitalis lanata	bumble-bee	15	4
D. lutea	bumble-bee	19·5	6·5
D. purpurea	bumble-bee	43	6
Primula kewensis	bee-fly	19	6
Plumbago rosea	butterfly	20·3	12·5
Jasminum primulinum	butterfly	13	5
Clerodendrum thomsonae	moth (?)	22	8·4
Jasminium polyanthum	moth (?)	27	10
Freesia refracta	moth	30	8·7
Eucharis grandiflora	moth	60	13·9
Datura sanguinea	moth	197	59
Grevillea rosmarinifolia	bird	9	4
Manettia inflata	bird	18	6
Billbergia nutans	bird	20·5	9
Leonotis leonurus	bird	31·75	6
Impatiens niamniamensis	bird (?)	33	20
Phormium tenax	bird	35	19
Aloë arborescens	bird	40	20·5
Musa velutina, male flower	bird or bat	40	18
Musa velutina hermaphrodite flowers	bird or bat	32	13

Hovering while probing is not invariable. Vogel (1954) states that when *Hippotion celerio*, the Silver-striped Hawkmoth, visits the orchid *Habenaria polyphylla*, it places its fore-feet on the right and left edges of the three-cornered rostellum. They come in contact with the glands of the pollinia which stick to its legs as it flies off. The moth may collect several pairs of pollinia on each foreleg and undoubtedly transfers pollen to other flowers. Its unusual trait of landing on the flower results in this special and successful method of pollination.

Posoqueria latifolia (Rubiaceae) is another long-tubed (15 cm) moth flower whose pollination mechanism is somewhat different. The anthers of the stamens are all connivent and deflected downwards before the mouth of the corolla tube, so that the filaments are strongly curved. The anthers dehisce introrsely, as in the daisies. When the moth inserts its tongue into the tube, the filaments spring apart and shower it with pollen, especially upon the tongue itself. This is essential for successful pollination because the forked stigma extends less than two-thirds up the very narrow corolla tube and the tongue alone can reach it (Cammerloher, 1930).

Moths appreciate scents in extreme dilution, the males even react to a single molecule of the females' mating scent (Ford, 1956). Kerner states that a moth liberated 100 yards away from a Honeysuckle bush, flew straight towards it, although it was out of sight. Scent then, is the foremost attractive attribute of the moth flower.

BUTTERFLY FLOWERS

Butterflies prefer to visit flowers with long narrow tubes and flat-topped corollas. These two features are prominent among their favourite plants which include *Buddleia variabilis*, different species of thistles, *Crocus vernus*, *Primula farinosa*, *Dianthus barbatus*, *Lychnis dioica*, *Lantana comosa* and various species of asclepias.

The butterfly's tongue is *dry*, *smooth* and very long and slender, and it is unlikely that it retains much pollen. If the stigmas and stamens are concealed within the corolla tube, as in *Buddleia* and *Lantana*, there is little possibility of it transferring pollen by means of its legs and feet. In these circumstances the butterfly effects "tongue-tip" pollination. In flowers such as thistles, *Crocus*, *Dianthus* and *Lychnis*, which have their anthers and stigmas exposed above the corolla tube, the likelihood of pollination is enhanced. Although butterflies appear at some disadvantage on shallow flowers, in *Geranium pyrenaicum* the slow deliberate movements of their legs among the stamens and styles result in an excellent distribution of the pollen up the whole length of the stigmas. More data on the transference of pollen between one flower and another are needed.

The Milkweed, *Asclepias syriaca* is associated with the Monarch or Milkweed Butterfly, *Danaus plexippus*, in North America. *Asclepias* has pollinia linked in pairs by a sticky gland which is situated midway between both the anthers and coronal cups and immediately above the narrow slit leading to the stigmas (Fig. 14). The gland is cleft, and wedge-shaped, and clamps firmly round the insect's leg, which latter slips naturally into the slit as the insect shifts its position while drinking the copious nectar in the coronal cups. When the insect pulls its leg out, the pollinia come away too and may be carried to other flowers. The weakness of this highly specialized mechanism is that it is too efficient. The butterfly has to exert considerable force to extricate its leg from the groove, and only the larger, stronger ones can do this. Others are trapped and flutter helplessly until they die. Many are caught by the proboscis and these too find difficulty in freeing themselves. They do not profit by experience, for, when they do become free, they will continue to visit the same species. In this they fall far short of the intelligent bees.

Primula farinosa is only pollinated by butterflies in the *alpine* regions of its range where the flowers are long-tubed. The lowland form of flower has a shorter, broader tube and is pollinated by bees.

Butterfly flowers are usually scented, yet Crane (1957) observed that recognition of *Lantana* is by *sight*. Three species of *Heliconius* failed to find the fragrant blooms if they were obscured by foliage, but flew immediately to the cluster if even a single flower was exposed to view.

The butterflies' seasons are geared to the food plants of their larvae rather than to the blooming of any species of flower. They usually have a long period of activity because more than one brood is reared. In the Simla hills (De Rhe-Philipe, 1931) the Painted Lady, *Vanessa cardui*, and the Red Admiral, *V. indica indica*, fly all the year round, but the former flies only in autumn and winter on the plains. Both species chiefly visit thistles in open scrubby country.

Butterflies resemble many flies and bumble-bees in exhibiting strong habitat preferences, some being found only in woods and the clearings therein, others like the *Vanessa* mentioned above ranging open country. The Blue Admiral, *V. canace himalaya* sticks near to streams.

Butterflies may assume an unwonted importance as pollinators under unusual climatic conditions. In South Africa, Vogel (1954) observed that during a drought there was a great increase in the number of butterflies paying visits to flowers, driven there by the need for water. No data are given as to whether a greater number of flowers were, in fact, pollinated.

Butterflies may be constant in their visits to a particular species or very erratic in their flower visits. A sharp contrast in behaviour is recorded by Christy, who saw *Vanessa*, *Colias*, *Parnassius* and *Pieris* make 75 per cent of their visits to a single species, and Bennett who found the same kinds making 78 per cent of *interspecific* visits (cited Grant, 1949). If they find a bountiful supply of nectar they tend to remain at the one source.

If we take into consideration the nature of the butterfly's tongue, the inconstancy of its flower visits and the absence of phenological links between them and the flowers themselves, we may agree with Robertson (1926) that the butterflies evolved later than the bees and have taken possession of the long-tongued bee flowers without having been involved in the fashioning of them.

POLLINATION BY WASPS

Wasps feed their young on animal food: insects, such as beetles and flies, and spiders. They do not collect or eat pollen, and only visit flowers for nectar. *Vespa* spp. in the British Isles and in North America, appear to be markedly selective and visit species of figwort, earning them the name of "wasp flowers". They are assiduous workers of both *Scrophularia nodosa* and *S. aquatica* (Water Betony) and virtually every flower is repeatedly entered and abundantly pollinated. Even solitary plants are found and worked to the last flower. The corolla is about 1 cm deep, and wide enough for the wasp to push its head down into it. The stigma is placed centrally in the mouth of the corolla, bending down and out of the lower lip as it ages. The nectar is copious and the concentration varies from 12·5–50 + per cent sugar. The plant has a strong unpleasant smell. The chocolaty-crimson flowers are relatively inconspicuous in both the above species. The yellow flowered *S. vernalis* flowers from April to June before worker wasps are abroad and is pollinated by bees.

Correvon and Pouyanne (1923) observed an unusual insect–flower relationship in Algeria. Here, the Mirror Ophrys, *Ophrys speculum*, is pollinated by the males of *Colpa aurea*. The female wasp has a russet brown head and antennae and its short wings are a deep metallic blue. This matches the colouring of the throat and blade of the labellum of the orchid. The flower is nectarless, and the females never visit it, but take their nectar from *Centaurea pullata*, *Galactites tomentosa* and *Malva sylvestris*. The males emerge a few days before the females, and, if the orchids are at hand, alight on the labellum and attempt to copulate with it. They successfully transfer the pollinia, for up to 40 per cent of the capsules set seed. As soon as the females appear, the visits to the orchid cease.

Hagerup (1932) reports a "big clumsy" wasp, *Eumenes tinctor* as a very abundant and very important pollinator of all the forest trees at Timbuctu. The chief species are the sweet-scented *Acacia tortilis* and *Zizyphus jujuba* (Rhamnaceae). The air is so hot that it is only bearable for insects at tree-top level, so that only these are insect pollinated. The ground flora is all cleistogamous.

POLLINATION BY BEETLES

A great many species of beetles visit flowers, but, in the great majority of cases, the plant reaps no benefit. Beetles eat pollen and anthers, lick up nectar from the exposed nectaries of the Umbelliferae or the shallow cups of the Golden-rod, *Solidago* spp., and gnaw any soft parts of the flower, especially the ovaries. This damage is often severe and is not offset by pollen transference, for pollen does not adhere well to the smooth wing cases and bodies of the beetles. Neither does their behaviour help for they tend to move very little between one flower and another, and their flight is erratic.

There are no flowers adapted to pollination by beetles, although there are cases of beetles effecting pollination. This is remarkable, for beetles were probably the earliest of the flower-visiting insects. They predate by some 200 million years the modern anthophilous groups of the bees and butterflies. As far back as the Carboniferous, Gymnosperms and Pteridosperms were producing "catkins" with abundant pollen, and the Mesozoic Bennettitales, had large pinnate stamens, which may have been eaten by beetles. Today, coniferous pollen is widely exploited, and the most primitive Angiosperm flower, the Magnolia is pollinated by beetles according to Delpino (1868–70) but these insects have not evolved a mutual beneficial association with any kind of flower. The Blister Beetles, *Gnathium* and *Nemognatha* have become completely adapted to work flowers with deep corollas. They have slender suctorial tongues, up to 11 mm in length, grooved like a butterfly's but incapable of being rolled up. They feed entirely on nectar but are probably just nectar thieves, as are some butterflies. The Cerambycidae show a series of species from those which never visit flowers to completely anthophilous forms. These latter tend to have narrow, elongated heads (narrowed to a neck behind the eyes), a narrow prothorax and a strong development of hairs on the lobes of the maxilla. These are probably not adaptations to flower visiting as these beetles are wood borers, and their whole body is slender and cylindrical. Their form is more truly adapted to their habitat.

190

Leptura livida is found chiefly on the flowers of the Umbelli-ferae, Rosaceae, Compositae, and *Convolvulus*. *Strangalia attenuata* is able to exploit the nectar of *Knautia arvensis*, Field Scabious, which is 4–5 mm deep. Many species of beetles, especially the wood borers are found in the shallow receptacles of the perigynous roses. Lovell records 31 species on Shadbush, *Amelanchier canadensis*, 43 on Chokecherry, *Prunus virginiana*, 42 on the Willow Spiraea, *Spiraea salicifolia*, 38 on *Cornus* sp. and 81 on the Sheepberry, *Viburnum lentago*. No data are available as to whether, and to what extent they effect pollination.

Delpino states that magnolia is fertilized exclusively by *Cetonia*, which feeds on the pollen and sweet juices of the flower. Very possibly *Arum nigrum* is beetle-pollinated for the foetid smell of the spathe attracts several kinds of dung and carrion beetle. They are found in quantity within the spathes. They include two Lamellicorn Dung Beetles, *Aphrodius* and *Ontho-phagus*, the former a scavenger and the latter a dungball beetle related to the Sacred Scarab of Ancient Egypt; and *Polydrusus* a brilliant metallic green weevil.

Lovell notes that the Blueflag Beetle, *Mononychus vulpeculus*, makes many punctures in the nectary of *Iris versicolor*, and the nectar which flows out attracts many other insects, especially flies. Are these instrumental in pollinating the flowers? McCann (1942) observed pollination by beetles in Indian species of *Lemna* and *Spirodela* (Duckweeds). Tiny weevils (Curculioni-dae) lay their eggs in the fronds and transfer pollen across the floating rafts of plants. There is provision for cross-pollination. Each minute inflorescence consists of two stamens and one carpel enclosed in a membraneous scale, the spathe. First one stamen elongates and dehisces, then the stigma becomes receptive and lastly the second stamen dehisces. *Lemna eleanorae* McCann has echinate pollen, a particular feature of insect-pollinated plants.

CHAPTER X

ISOLATING
MECHANISMS IN
FLOWERS

GRANT (1949) showed that there are two kinds of isolating mechanisms in flowers which may prevent cross-pollination between two related species, even though they are interfertile and grow together in the same locality. Both depend on the capabilities and behaviour of the flower visitors. Firstly, there is **mechanical** isolation which exists where the floral mechanisms of the two species differ, so that an insect can operate the one and not the other. Secondly, there is **ethological** isolation, where cross-pollination is mechanically possible, but does not occur because the visitors are highly selective, and visit the one form to the exclusion of the other. This flower constancy is a marked feature of bee behaviour.

MECHANICAL ISOLATION

There are many instances of mechanical isolation among moth, butterfly and bee plants. Differences in corolla shape, strength, depth or width may each and all create barriers which cannot be surmounted by some would be visitors. The Bluebell, *Endymion non-scriptus*, has a long narrow bell, 1·5–2 cm, formed of closely overlapping perianth segments (**tepals**). Although they are unjoined, the honey-bee cannot force its way into the bell far enough to reach the nectar. It resorts to stealing it by slipping its tongue between the base of the tepals. The Spanish

Bluebell, *E. hispanicus*, has a spreading bell, wide enough for the bees to enter and work legitimately. This mechanical barrier probably limits the extent of cross-pollination between the two species, for the chance of pollen being transferred from the former to the latter is slight, unless the bees are working both plants for pollen. Hybrids do occur, so the barrier is only partial.

There is potentially a mechanical barrier to **intraspecific** pollination in *Glechoma hederacea*. The species is **gynodioecious** and this is coupled with floral dimorphism. The hermaphrodite flowers are twice the size of the female flowers, both in breadth of petals and tube length (Figs. 4 and 5) (see Chapter I); indeed the former appear to be too deep for the honey-bee, while the latter are just the right length. This may lead to preferential visiting of the two plants and reduce the seed set of the female plant.

Both inter- and intra-specific mechanical barriers exist between *Platanthera chlorantha* and *P. bifolia*, the Greater and Lesser Butterfly Orchids. Both of them have whitish, sweet-scented flowers, narrow strap shaped labellums, and long, very slender spurs which secrete nectar. The first mechanical barrier is the exceedingly narrow bore of the spurs. These are only about 1 mm in diameter, and this prevents any insect, other than a lepidopteran from probing them. Then comes the barrier between the species themselves. The spur of *P. bifolia* is 15–20 mm long, that of *P. chlorantha*, 19–28 mm. This difference is sufficient to stratify the insect visitors: the former is visited by the Treble Bar, *Anaites plagiata* (Hydriomenidae), and the Turnip Moth, *Agrotis segetum*, which receive the pollinia on the base of the tongue, the latter by "Y" Moths, *Plusia* sp, and *Hadena dentina* (Noctuidae), the pollinia sticking to the side of the head. Lastly, the intra-specific barrier: on the continent *P. chlorantha*, has spurs from 23–43 mm in length. The longest ones are beyond the reach of the Noctua and can only be exploited by Sphingids.

The length of the corolla tube, rather than the width, acts as a barrier to visitors to *Trifolium* spp. The honey-bee, and even the short-tongued bees such as *Andrena* and *Halictus*, are able to work White Clover, *T. repens*, but the longer flowers of *T. medium*, 18 mm, *T. incarnatum*, 9–15 mm; and Red Clover *T. pratense*, 15–18 mm; completely screen out the two solitary bees and the honey-bee too, as far as nectar is concerned, leaving these flowers to the long tongued bumble-bees. As in *Platanthera chlorantha*, the length of the corolla tube stratifies visitors in Red Clover. Hawkins (1961) has demonstrated quite different species patterns of bee visitors to different commercial strains, which have different corolla lengths.

In *Antirrhinum*, the strength required to depress the lower lip of the personate corolla excludes most insects and isolates the plant mechanically from all but the strong and heavy bumble-bees. There are even stouter barriers in the Carpenter-bee flowers (see Chapter IX).

ETHOLOGICAL ISOLATION

Ethological isolation occurs at **subspecific** levels in Gilia (Grant, 1949). *Gilia capitata capitata* and *G. capitata tomentosa* have pale lavender flowers and a sweet scent. *G. capitata chamissonis* has deep blue violet flowers and smells of creosote. The shape of the corolla also varies. *G. c. capitata* has narrow pointed petals, *G. c. tomentosa* has broader ones and those of *G. c. chamissonis* are twice as broad as *G. c. tomentosa*. The nectar of all is available to the honey-bee. The bee will probably be able to distinguish between the two colours (see Colour Vision). It will perceive the difference in scent, and possibly of form. Eighty plants of these three subspecies were randomized in a plot and the honey-bee visitors watched. If a bee visited *G. c. chamissonis* first, it remained constant to it, although it would approach the flowers of the other two. Other bees visiting either of the other two subspecies first, would afterwards work freely, between them, virtually ignoring *G. c. chamissonis*. This isolation held during the spring: later in the summer, some bees working *G. c. capitata* and *G. c. tomentosa* occasionally visited *G. c. chamissonis*, and vice versa. To confirm the visual data, seedlings of the three strains were raised and classed as subspecies or hybrids. The two parents *G. c. capitata* and *G. c. tomentosa* produced no hybrids with *G. c. chamissonis*, so the bees brought no pollen from the latter to the two former plants. The parent *G. c. chamissonis* produced 19·6 per cent of hybrids with *G. c. tomentosa* and 2·1 per cent with *G. c. capitata*. *G. c. capitata* showed 58·7 per cent hybrids with *G. c. tomentosa* as might have been predicted. Crossings between the subspecies are not fully compatible and only produce half the number of seeds that selfing does, so the bees must have made more visits between the subspecies than the results show.

An ethological barrier may be raised between the thrum-eyed and pin-eyed flowers of the self-sterile *Primula elatior*, if bumble-bees are the *only* visitors, for, if pollen collecting, they learn to recognize the latter at a distance and avoid them.

Grant, on analysis of 416 genera of all pollination classes, finds that the taxonomic differences between species which are non-promiscuously pollinated, are mostly characters relating to flower form. This is particularly the case in flowers pollinated by bees and birds. Anemophilous plants on the other hand, show relatively few taxonomic characters relating to the flower; for example, the oaks (*Quercus* spp.) are separated chiefly by vegetative characters such as leaf form. This strongly suggests that floral isolating mechanisms have been operating extensively and for a long time during the evolution of the Angiosperms and have played an important role in speciation. He outlines a mechanism by which this might be accomplished. He postulates the appearance of a recessive mutant strain, differing from the parent in one or more floral characters. A few bees might become fixed to these mutant plants, but, because their number would be few, would probably move out to the type plants to complete their foraging. Bees have a habit of returning to the first plant they forage on subsequent trips, so they would tend to carry the pollen of the mutant back to the parent strain, and thereby increase the genetical possibility of more of the mutant individuals appearing in the progeny. With a fair number of mutant plants to forage, some bees might confine their attentions entirely to them and help to stabilize them as a distinct population. At present, the evidence points the other way. Ethological isolation appears to keep compatible species, which are growing together, very separate from one another. It is, however, worth noting that Goetze (1930) has found that the *white* flowered sports of Red Clover, *Trifolium pratense*, Crimson Clover, *T. incarnatum* and Alfalfa, *Medicago sativa*, all secrete more nectar than the coloured flowers. If the nectar too, were more concentrated than that of the type, there would be a possibility of the mechanism outlined above functioning.

OTHER ISOLATING MECHANISMS

Compatible species may be isolated **phenologically**. The orchadist mitigates this in fruit varieties by devices such as the cold storage of pollen. *Agrostis tenuis*, the Common Bent Grass, cannot interbreed with the Brown Bent, *A. canina*, because they flower at different times of the day (and grass pollen does not remain long in the air). Anther dehiscence in *A. tenuis* occurs in the morning, and in *A. canina* in the evening.

BREEDING SYSTEMS IN THE FLOWERING PLANTS

In order to assess the value of our floral biological observations on a species, it is necessary to know something of its genetic constitution and breeding system. This is an essential preliminary step in the investigation of any species. For instance, it would be unprofitable to determine the extent to which cross-pollination was occurring between **apomictic** individuals (see below). The following remarks only indicate a few of the characteristics of the breeding systems. In order to grasp the fundamentals, the student should refer to genetical works such as *The Evolution of Genetic Systems*, by C. A. Darlington. Students should also consult *The Chromosome Atlas of Flowering Plants*, by Darlington and Wylie, and also the indices of genetical journals for published work on the species in which they are interested.

Any species which is to survive and evolve needs a genetic make-up in which a balance is present between *fitness* and *flexibility*. Fitness will enable it to succeed in its present environment, and flexibility will enable its progeny, or at least some of them, to respond to any new conditions to which they may be subjected by a change in climate, or which they may meet on immigrating to a fresh site. The greater the stability of the genetic constitution, the greater the uniformity between the plants in the population, and the better they will succeed in their present environment.

Flexibility is attained by maintaining a considerable degree of hybridity in the population. Its physical basis is the interchange of parts of chromosomes, which occurs at pairing, during meiosis, and which has, as its result the recombination of linked characters. Flexibility can only be increased at the expense of the general fitness of the population, for some members will show characters which are either unnecessary for life in their present environment, or which may even be in varying degree deleterious.

The genetic constitution is influenced by the breeding system of the species. **Outbreeding**, by means of cross fertilization, is the normal and most common type in the flowering plants, and this system gives the greatest possibilities for recombination and for maintaining genetic variability, that is, it gives the maximum flexibility. It is ensured in many ways, by offering abundant insect food to attract pollinators; by floral devices which prevent self-pollination; by different sex distributions; by self sterility; by heteromorphy coupled with genetic factors which influence the growth of the pollen tubes in the stylar tissue.

Inbreeding reduces the amount of genic material available for recombination, but may result in greater individual fitness, as when a small population is isolated geographically, forced to inbreed, and certain of its progeny are preferentially selected in that particular ecological niche.

Stebbins (1950) points out that if insects are scarce, or the plants are growing very far apart, self-pollination, coupled with self-fertility (autogamy), is an advantage. It will maintain the species until such time as it is thicker on the ground, or until it may be able to benefit from a peak in the population of a pollinating insect. Annual plants, which rely on an abundant production of seed to enable them to colonize any temporary bare ground rapidly and in strength, are very often self-pollinated. Here, the fitness of the individual to survive and colonize, is more important than flexibility, for if no seed is produced in any season the species survival may be seriously jeopardized.

The breeding system of a species has different potentialities in different situations. Palmer (1962) has shown that the composition of the population affects the number of hybrid plants which will be produced. For example, a Turnip plant, *Brassica campestris*, which is self-sterile, will form up to 88 per cent of hybrids when growing isolated in a crop of Rape, *B. napus*; but there is little difference in the number of hybrids produced by the self-fertile Rape plants growing among Turnips, whatever proportion of the crop they form and however they may be distributed in it.

APOMIXIS

Some species have become apomictic; that is, the ovule develops into a seed without being fertilized. This is easily demonstrated in the Common Dandelion, *Taraxacum officinale*, by cutting off the stamens and styles just prior to flowering: the head will set good fruit. Fertilization is secured by internal means: the egg becomes diploid by the fusion with a sister nucleus, or by the failure of the reduction division, or by some other means. When a species becomes apomictic, the maintenance of genetical variability by means of recombination comes to an end. It will be able to survive if suited to its habitat Apomixis does not necessarily bring the evolution of the species to an end, for each apomictic individual will retain and perpetuate its own variability in its offspring and these may be subject to selection. If it is a **facultative** apomict, able to exchange genic material by occasionally producing a sexual generation, then it may achieve a balance between stability and flexibility which is advantageous and will permit adaptation. This happens in some species of *Taraxacum* and then the flower's obsolescent, but first-class mechanism for cross-pollination, comes into play again. (Cross-pollination, in the Composites, is ensured by the piston mechanism of the style through the anther box which enables the pollen to be presented first; and then follows the spreading of the two stigmas well above their own pollen). It is backed up by a rich pollen with a high fat content, which is particularly attractive to honeybees, and also by a nectar with a high sugar content. Here then, is a double safeguard; firstly the sporadic appearance of sexual plants, and secondly retention of the cross-pollinating mechanism.

Floral biological safeguards occur in other plants. The orchids, as a whole, have attained a higher degree of specialization for insect pollination than any other group. The number of species is second only to the daisies, but nowhere are they a dominant feature of the vegetation. Some of the British terrestrial orchids now suffer from lack of pollinators. *Ophrys apifera*, the Bee Orchid, has a pouched labellum resembling, in shape and markings, a bumble-bee, and perhaps was pollinated by pseudocopulation with some male insect, but it seems to have lost its pollinator altogether. Two sessile stigmas lie at the back of the opening to the pouch, and immediately above them is a single anther. The pollen within each anther lobe is cemented together into a single mass, or **pollinium**, and attached by a slender tail of tissue, the **caudicle** to a sticky knob. The knob is on the front of a protruding pad of tissue called the **rostellum**. In other orchids, and potentially in this one, the knobs become cemented to some part of the visitors' body, the head or the proboscis, and, in backing away, the insect draws out the pollinia and carries them off to another flower. This species is now self-pollinated. The two pollinia are pulled from their anther lobes by the shrinkage of their caudicles. They droop out of the lobe, and, as they hang just above the stigmatic patches, are easily brought into contact with them by the wind (Fig. 66).

Different species of *Epipactis* show a gradation from insect pollination to apomixy. *E. palustris* is successfully and abundantly pollinated by the honey-bee: the flowers contain nectar, the labellum stands out to form a landing place, the tepals open fully. *E. pendula* has no nectar, the flowers are pendulous and self-pollinating. *E. vectensis* is semi-cleistogamous, which is a stage towards self-fertilization, but the **column**, which bears the anther rostellum, degenerates in the bud stage, so autogamy is impossible. This species is probably apomictic, which makes it independent of a pollinator, but it has forfeited the chance of further outbreeding by losing its cross-pollinating mechanism. The Dandelion is in better case.

Members of the Lobelioid group of the Lobeliaceae lost their only pollinators in areas where the Hawaiian Honey-creepers, Drepanididae, became extinct. The birds had bills of the right proportions to probe the flower tubes. These plants, one is *Cyanea hirtella* Rock, are persisting and setting seed having successfully reverted to autogamy.

FIG. 66. *Ophrys apifera*, the Bee Orchid. A pollinium dangling on its slender caudicle before the mouth of the flower, whence it is blown by the wind onto the sessile stigma. ×2.

The "clip" and "slot" device of *Asclepias* traps and kills all but the strongest butterflies and limits cross-pollination. Asa Gray observed skeins of pollen tubes issuing from the anther, but it was not seen whether they grew into the slot and reached the stigma. Occasionally, in species which are self-sterile, the stigmas' power of inhibiting the germination of its "own" pollen, may vary during the flowering period and some flowers show "end of season" self compatibility, which is in the nature of a biological safeguard.

UNFAVOURABLE ENVIRONMENTAL CONDITIONS

Facultative cleistogamy is a safety device, widespread among plant families, which is brought into play by abnormal environmental conditions. For this safeguard to work, the flowers have, of necessity, to be self-fertile. The flowers produced during unfavourable periods may differ very little from the chasmogams, for example, a Water Buttercup, in time of flood, will fail to open, but it is not otherwise modified. In regions where conditions are extremely rigorous, as at Timbuctu, the ground flora is almost exclusively cleistogamous and self-pollinated. Some of the flowers are highly modified as in *Commelina forskålei* Vahl (Chapter I).

Ulex europaeus begins to flower very early in the spring when the honey-bees are often unable to forage regularly because of the low temperatures. Flowers, opening in February, may wait weeks before being pollinated. During this time, the standard petal which is originally raised, becomes full grown and flattened onto the keel, but it is not clamped down tightly around it. The edges of the standard remain level or are slightly curved upwards. This is all that is required to permit the bee to gain the necessary foothold to lever it up again and spring the flower. After springing, the standard lowers onto the bud, but now its edges flatten down the sides of the keel and further exploitation is so difficult that the bees seldom attempt it. So the flowers do not lose anything through the vagaries of the spring weather, and their pollen is kept intact ready for a sunny day.

In *Veronica persica*, on a warm dry morning in the spring, the new flowers open early and the filaments rapidly extend to their full length in the familiar lateral position on either side of the stigma and well away from it (as in *V. gentianoides*, Fig. 57). Dehiscence then takes place. On dull damp mornings in the autumn and winter, the anthers remain clasping hands, as it were, over the stigma and dehisce *before* parting, so that the flowers are self-pollinated. A good set of seed capsules may be found at almost any time of the year.

In their natural alpine habitat, *Saxifraga cernua* and *Polygonum viviparum* produce very few flowers. Except for the terminal flowers on the inflorescence, which are normal, each of the floral bracts has a bulbil in its axil. The bulbil of *P. vivi-parum* is a tiny blackish nut, those of the Saxifrage are red and occur in groups. It may be that the environment is unsuitable for seed development and that bulbil production is a biological

Fig. 67a. *Iris pseudacorus.* Freshly opened flower with petaloid styles held 1 cm above the fall tepals. In this stage it is pollinated by bumble-bees. × 1·1.

safeguard, but those of the *Polygonum* are a favourite food of Ptarmigan, so it may not benefit much. It is unlikely to be due to lack of pollinators, for the almond-scented protandrous, terminal flowers of *S. cernua* are visited by flies. Moreover, they are orientated towards the incident light, and this is generally favourable to pollination, yet seed is unknown.

Movement of the flower parts may alter and enhance the

chance of pollination. Muller (1893) observed that *Iris pseudacorus* has two forms of flower; one in which the petaloid styles are held well above the fall, and one where they are almost touching the falls (Fig. 67). The first kind was largely pollinated by bumble-bees, whereas the second was almost exclusively visited by the long-tongued Hover-fly, *Rhingia rostrata* (proboscis 11 mm). The altitude of the style is a function of flower

FIG. 67b.   *Iris pseudacorus*.   One-day-old flower with styles lowered to within 2–3 mm of falls. In this stage it is pollinated by *Rhingia rostrata*.   × 1·1.

age. The flowers last 1–1·5 days: when they first open, the styles are held high, about 1 cm above the falls, then they gradually lower until only a 2–3 mm gap is left between them. This is another kind of biological safeguard, the flowers having the chance of pollination by insects of very different sizes during their short life. One may note that the more efficient and energetic insect is catered for first. The case of *Acanthus mollis* is similar to that of Iris. In the Mediterranean region, it is pollinated by *Xylocopa* (see Carpenter-bee Flowers), which is strong enough to shoulder apart the anthers and receive the pollen on its back; but the flowers are successfully pollinated in Britain by *Bombus agrorum* workers because the style curls down bringing the stigma near to the lower petal. The yellow and blue Forget-me-not, *Myosotis discolor* also has a device for self-pollination. In the young flower, the stigma protrudes from the corolla: the anthers are below within the tube. As the flower ages, the corolla tube elongates and brings the anthers level with the stigma.

FLORAL BIOLOGY — LINKS WITH OTHER DISCIPLINES

Floral biology is intimately linked with other biological disciplines, and only lack of workers in this field prevent it contributing its full share. Autecological studies of a plant species include almost no floral biological data except the period of flowering. Usually there is a list of the insects found on the flowers, but seldom is there any assessment of their value as pollinators.

There is a vast field in the ecology of pollination awaiting investigation, and the findings might help to solve many problems of ecology and distribution.

Floral biology is widely applied in agriculture, particularly in relation to the production of commercial seed crops such as Red Clover, Alfalfa and brassicas. For example, varieties of brassica in East Anglia are planted in zones, a minimal 1000 yd apart, to prevent cross-pollination; and Early-flowering Red Clover is now cut in June, for hay, in order to delay flowering until late July, when there are enough bumble-bee workers for pollination. But the necessity of providing nesting sites for the bumble-bees, and adequate forage for them both before and after they are needed to pollinate the crop is less often appreciated. In some areas, particularly in the U.S.A., agricultural practice, (such as planting crops in large blocks with the consequent elimination of hedges and rough ground, the spraying of weeds and the close cutting of pastures by modern machinery which destroys the bees' nests) has already reduced the wild-bee population to below the level necessary for an adequate seed yield. The orchardist requires an intimate knowledge of the floral biology of his varieties of fruit in order to plan and plant successfully. Detailed data of the biology of the stigma and pollen is vital to the plant breeder.

CHAPTER XI

PRACTICAL WORK IN FLORAL BIOLOGY

WE DO not know the complete floral biology of any species of plant. Some economic crops, the clovers, alfalfa, cotton, cucumbers and oranges have attracted considerable attention, but even for these the data are incomplete. This means that any observer may amass original data and add to our knowledge in this field. This will be all the more valuable if observations on both the plant and its visitors run concurrently. The following schedule sketches briefly some profitable lines of investigation. Then follow notes on procedure and the making and use of some essential equipment. There is no technique beyond the capability of anyone, provided she or he has patience, good eyesight and a delicate touch.

SCHEDULE

Observations of Flowers

Choose a species near at hand which you can conveniently study.

Object

To ascertain the pollination potential in all its aspects.

Suggested Lines of Study

1. *Phenology* of flowers, i.e. dates of first opening, peak of flowering, last flowers.

2. *Study of flower form*, i.e. shape, dimensions, colour, scent.

3. *Presence of insect food*, i.e. nectar, pollen, fodder hairs.

4. *Availability of insect food*, i.e. depth at which nectar is situated. Presentation of pollen.

5. *Times at which food is available.*

6. *Quality and quantity of food*, i.e. amount of pollen and nectar, concentration of nectar.

7. *Insect visitors*, identification, behaviour, result of visit.

Observations of Insects

At the Crop

1. *Identification of visitor.*

2. *Time of visit*; also note weather conditions.

3. *Marking*; method described in text.

4. *Technique employed by visitor.*

5. *Efficiency as a pollinator.* (a) result of visit; pollination? damage? theft? (b) number of flowers visited. (c) length of visit.

Notes. Mark insect immediately it arrives at crop. Use stop watch to record length of visit. Marking is easiest *early* in day when insects are not so active and spend longer at each flower.

Recording. It is often profitable for two students to work together, especially when observing insects whose movements may be rapid, one worker keeping the insect continually under observation and calling out the data for his partner to record. If you have to work alone, use a tape recorder and microphone on a long flex to permit you to move about.

Period of Observations. These may have to be limited to suit the convenience of the worker and may necessitate covering the crop before work begins. Bags made from Terylene or Polythene may be used but remember that condensation is a problem in the latter.

The Biology of the Pollinating Insects. Students who have access to a hive of bees or a nest of bumble-bees will have the benefit of making detailed observations of two very important pollinating insects which are otherwise not easily obtainable. Bumble-bees are easy to keep and take up very little room on a bench, and the only entrance needed for them is a piece of strong tubing through a crack in the window. Detailed instructions for finding and taking the nest, building the nest-box and the subsequent care of the colony, is admirably described in Free and Butler's book on bumble-bees. One modification of their nest-box which is recommended is the provision of a small sliding panel in the partition between the nestchamber and the antechamber, and also between the antechamber and the exit tube. This enables the bees to be temporarily confined to the nest and returning foragers to be shut out if necessary. Data of bumble-bee biology are badly needed.

The Pocket Spectrometer and its use. The *concentration* of the nectar in a flower is probably the most important single factor influencing the visits of pollinators, especially if they be insects. The pocket spectrometer, which gives a direct reading of the percentage of sugar in the nectar, is ideal for field work. Most nectars range between 5 per cent and 45 per cent of solids (sugars), so the instrument spanning the 0–50 per cent range for *sugars* is the best type to buy. The advantage of this kind of instrument is that only a very small amount of fluid is needed for sampling. The close-fitting prisms spread even a minute drop of nectar sufficiently to obtain an accurate reading. Instructions for the use of the instrument are supplied with it, but one point needs particular attention. The *faces of the prisms are very delicate* and liable to be scratched. Clean them only with moistened lens tissue and use a light touch. If placing a drop of nectar on the prism from a pipette, hold the latter *parallel with the surface* of the prism and let the drop well out of the tip and contact the face *sideways.* This will prevent damage to the prism by accidental contact with the tip of the pipette.

THE TECHNIQUE OF EXPLOITING FLOWERS FOR NECTAR

1. *Making the pipettes.* You will need some glass capillator tubing in short lengths such as is supplied with the standard capillator sets for measuring pH. Turn a bunsen flame very low—about $1\frac{1}{2}$ in. is ideal—and see that there is no yellow in the flame (you do not want unburnt carbon on your pipette). Grasp the tube at each end and hold the centre part in the tip of the flame until it begins to wobble. Remove it from the flame and, as you do so, pull apart firmly but not too swiftly. A thin

filament some 4–5 in. in length should be formed in the middle of the tube. Allow to cool and then break into two. Examine the end of the pipette with a lens to see if it has snapped directly at right angles to its length. If the end is slanting, or has a rough lip, it is impossible to remove the nectar completely with it; moreover, there is a danger of piercing the tissue of the flower with the uneven end. This should never happen; the nectar should not be contaminated with plant juices. Small rubber teats to fit the end of the pipette are supplied with the pH set, or can be bought separately, as can the tubing.

2. *Sampling.* Flowers should be absolutely fresh—even slight wilting makes them virtually impossible to handle. Loss of turgor renders the petal tissues so delicate that the pipette breaks through them instead of being guided along their curves to the nectar. Ideally, the flowers should not be removed from the plant. Fix the teat to barrel end of the pipette. Partially exhaust the teat by pressing between finger and thumb, then probe gently to the base of the flower. Release the pressure of the fingers on the teat *very gradually* when the nectar will flow up into the capillary of the pipette. Do not fill more than 1 cm of the barrel with nectar or it will be impossible to remove the teat without sucking nectar up into it. The nectar will not flow out of the capillary if it is withdrawn a millimetre or so from the tip and then kept in a horizontal position.

Some flowers with very long or curved tubes cannot be exploited by a glass pipette. It may be quicker and easier to pull off the corolla and express the nectar by gentle pressure with the fingers onto the refractometer. Fortunately, very little nectar is lost by doing this as it mostly adheres to the corolla, but there is a danger of expressing plant juices if the tube is squeezed tightly.

The Torsion Balance. If you wish to ascertain the amount as well as the percentage of sugar in the nectar, this direct reading balance is indispensable, for the speed of handling and recording samples is a limiting factor to the amount of work you can accomplish. A 0–500 mg model is most generally useful as it will weigh a single pollen ball or a pipette with nectar in it. Instructions for use are provided with the instrument. It is essential that it be placed on a level and firm base away from draughts. Never place a load on the hook without first locking the instrument and always release the locking lever very slowly to avoid dislodging the load. Never overload; the best weight to aim at is near the centre of the instrument's range. To weigh pipettes, construct a carriage for them by bending a piece of fuse wire into a V and turning the ends up. This will hang from the loading hook. By weighing the pipette before and after use, one can find the weight of nectar in mg, then the percentage of sugar is ascertained with the spectrometer. Small silver paper cups, made by smoothing the paper over the end of a pencil, are useful for weighing pollen and pollen pellets, or larger samples of nectar.

Pollen collection by bees. One may watch bees collecting pollen from flowers in the field, but to obtain an all-round picture of their activities, it is necessary to observe them as they return from foraging.

OBSERVATIONS AT THE HIVE MOUTH

1. *Precautions.* It is essential that the observer be completely protected against the possibility of being stung. A boiler-suit or slacks with the legs tucked into wellington boots and topped by a long jacket or light raincoat should be worn. Wear also a broad-brimmed hat with a bee veil with a ring of wire sewn in just above shoulder level to hold the net away from the face if it is windy. Tuck the ends of the veil well down into the collar of the coat. The best covering for the hands is a pair of household gloves of *thin* rubber, pulled up over the cuffs and secured with a rubber band. It is a good practice to dab a drop of T.C.P. or other mild disinfectant on the upper lip just below the nostrils; bees abhor the smell of human breath. These precautions may appear extreme to the experienced beeman, but unless one is confident and comfortable, one works slowly.

2. *Procedure.* Quietly place a low stool close beside the hive, level with (*but not in front of*) the alighting board. If you are right-handed the stool should be on the right of the hive (viewed from behind) and to the left if you are left-handed. Check that you have pen or pencil, watch, recording sheets, dissecting needle and a narrow strip of queen excluder (2×17 in.).

Spread a sheet of Polythene or place a tray on the ground in front of the alighting board to catch pollen pellets. Take your place a few minutes before you want to begin recording, and sit quietly watching the alighting board. You may see bees engaged in their dances "on the flat" and may be able to interpret them and learn the whereabouts of the crops they are working. The dancing bee can be marked on the thorax with a spot of quick-drying paint (choose a *light* colour, as it is more easily seen), and you may actually find her on the crop if you have read the dance aright. *On no account touch the wings with paint* or the bee will become unbalanced and unable to fly.

Make a note of the different colours of the pollen loads being carried in. If there are more than two, you will probably need a co-worker. Decide between you which colours you will watch for, one taking, say, the orange and the yellow, the other the blue and brown loads. When you think you have "got your eye in", prop the piece of queen excluder in front of the entrance, it is not necessary to fix it, and count the loads brought in over a period of, say, 4 or 5 min. After this the excluder should be removed to prevent too great a congestion of bees on the flight board. The excluder will slow up the bees sufficiently to permit of fairly easy and accurate counting. The observer should not take his eyes off the board while counting. If the recording sheet is divided into big squares, one for each colour, the hand will quickly accommodate itself to marking a stroke in the correct one without the worker glancing at the sheet. Mechanical counters may also be used. Observations may be repeated each hour or as often as is desired.

3. *Collecting samples.* As the bees crawl through the excluder some of the pollen loads become detached or can easily be removed by a gentle but firm stroke down the leg with a needle or grass stalk. Let them roll off the board onto the sheet below. The "catch" may then be sorted into colours and weighed if need be.

4. *Preparing the pollen for identification.* Pollen grains have to be fully expanded before identification is possible. To attain this: place a small heap of pollen (about $\frac{1}{4}$ of a pellet) at the centre of a microscope slide. Add a drop of absolute alcohol.

211

This will spread out, taking with it the oil from the pollen coat. Wipe the oily ring away and repeat the process. Then, before the pollen has time to dry, place a drop of 50 per cent glycerine on top. After a minute wipe most of this away and add a drop of pure glycerine. Melt some glycerine jelly, tinged *slightly* pink with Basic Fuchsin, in a pot in a warm water bath. Wipe away as much glycerine from the pollen as is possible, and put a drop of hot jelly on it. Place a coverslip on top and gently warm the slide until the jelly runs out to the edge of the coverslip. Ring with nail varnish. The pollen grains will pick up the pink stain, leaving the jelly colourless; this enables their structure to be seen easily.

5. *Identification.* Pollen fresh from the flowers and pellets collected by the bees may be matched and identified. Generally it is quite easy to find out which plants are being worked, as bees usually forage for pollen within $\frac{1}{4}$–$\frac{1}{2}$ mile of their hive or nest, but students will find Hodges *The Pollen Loads of the Honey-bee* an invaluable aid to identification. The accurate colour charts of pollen pellets are especially helpful and morphological details of individual grains are also given.

Students are advised to keep full and accurate notes of all their findings. Observations should be written up each day and all the data critically assessed, so that one may be able to spot any trends which may be developing. Then one is able to devise side experiments or take extra observations to confirm these before the season ends.

REFERENCES

ALPATOV, W. W. (1929) Biometrical studies on variation and races of the honeybee (*Apis mellifica*). *Quart. Rev. Biol.*, **41**, 1.

BERLIOZ, J. (1956) Sunbirds and hummingbirds. *J. Bombay Nat. Hist. Soc.*, **53**, 4, 515–522.

BEUTLER, R. and WAHL, O. (1936) Über das Honigen der Linde in Deutschland. *Z. vergl. Physiol.*, **23**, 301–331.

BEUTLER, R. and SCHÖNTAG, A. (1940) Über die Nektarabscheidung einiger Nutzpflanzen. *Z. vergl. Physiol.*, **28**, 254–285.

BEUTLER, R. (1953) Nectar. *Bee World*, **34**, 6, 7 and 8.

BEUTLER, R., VON CZARNOWSKI, C. and SHUEL, R. (1957) Report of working group on nectar research. *Bee World*, **38**, 2, 41.

BÖHNER, P. (1934) Zur Thermonastie der Tulpenblüte. *Ber. d. bot. Gesell*, **52**, 336.

BRIAN, A. D. (1957) Differences in flowers visited by four species of bumblebees and their causes. *J. Anim. Ecol.*, **26**.

BURCK, W. (1890) Über Kleistogamie im weitesten Sinne und das Knight–Darwinische gesetz. *Ann. Jard. Bot. Buitenz.*, **8**, 129–145.

BURKHARDT, D. and WENDLER, L. (1960) Ein direkter Beweis für die Fähigkeit einzelner Sehzellen des Insektenauges, die Schwingungsrichtung polarisierten Lichtes zu analysieren. *Z. vergl. Physiol.*, **43**, 6, 687–692.

BUTLER, C. G., JEFFREE, E. P. and KALMUS, H. (1943) The behaviour of a population of honeybees on an artificial and on a natural crop. *J. Exp. Biol.*, **20**, 65–73.

BUTLER, C. G. (1945) The behaviour of bees when foraging. *J. Roy. Soc. Arts*, **93**, 501.

CHAPMAN, F. M. (1926) The distribution of bird life in Ecuador. *Bull. Amer. Mus. Nat. Hist.*, **55**, 1.

COCKERELL, T. D. A. (1934) The wild bees. *Nat. Hist.* **34**, 748–753.

CORREVON and POUYANNE (1923) Nouvelles observations sur le mimetisme et la fécondation chez les *Ophrys speculum* et *lutea* (1). *J. Soc. Nat. Hort. France*, **24**, 372–377.

CRANE, J. (1957) Keeping house for tropical butterflies. *Nat. Geog. Mag.*, **122**, 2, 193–217.

DAUMER, K. (1958) Blumenfarben: wie sie die Bienen sehen. *Z. vergl. Physiol.* **41**, 49–110.

DELPINO, F: Ulteriori osservazioni sulla dicogamia nel regno vegetale. I (1868, 1869), II (1870, 1875) *Atti della Soc. Ital. delle Sc. Nat.*, **11**, 12.

DORMER, K. J. (1960) The truth about pollination in *Arum. New Phyt.*, **59**, 298–301.

FAHN, A. (1949) Studies in the ecology of nectar secretion. *Palest. J. Bot.* Jerusalem, **4**, 207–224.

FREE, J. B. (1962) Studies on the pollination of fruit trees by honeybees. *J. R. Hort. Soc.*, **87**, 302–309.

FREY-WYSSLING, A., ZIMMERMANN, M. and MAURIZIO, A. (1954) Über den enzymatischen Zuckerumbau in Nektarien. *Experientia*, **10**, 490–491.

FURGALA, B., GOCHNAUER, T. A. and HOLDAWAY, F. G. (1958) Constituent sugars of some northern legume nectars. *Bee World*, **39**, 203–5.

GANIER, A. F. (1957) Observations on ruby-throated hummingbirds. *The Migrant*, **28**, 3, 36–39.

GOETZE, G. (1930) Chemische und biologische Prüfung von Bienentrachtpflanzen. *Bienenweide* (A. Koch) 20 ed. Leipzig Bienenztg.

GRANT, V. (1949) Pollination systems as isolating mechanisms in Angiosperms. *Evol.*, **3**, 82–97.

HAGERUP, O. (1932) On pollination in the extremely hot air at Timbuctu. *Dansk. Bot. Ark.*, **8**, 1, 1–20.

HAGERUP, O. (1950) Rain pollination. *Dan. Biol. Medd.*, **18**, 5.

HAGERUP, O. (1951) Pollination in the Faroes, in spite of rain and poverty in insects. *Dan. Biol. Medd.*, **18**, 15.

HAWKINS, R. P. (1956) A preliminary survey of red clover seed production. *Ann. Appl. Biol.*, **44**, 657–664.

HAWKINS, R. P., (1961) Observations on the pollination of red clover by bees. I. The yield of seed in relation to the numbers and kinds of pollinators. *Ann. Appl. Biol.*, **49**, 55–65.

HESLOP-HARRISON, J. (1957) The sexuality of flowers. *New Biology* (Penguin Books), **23**, 9–28.

HYDE, H. A. and WILLIAMS, D. A. (1945) Pollen of Lime (*Tilia* spp.). *Nature*, **155**, 457–458.

HYDE, H. A. and WILLIAMS, D. A. (1946) Studies in atmospheric pollen III. Pollen and pollen incidence in ribwort plantain (*Plantago lanceolata* L.) *New Phytol.*, **45**, 271–277.

ILSE, D. (1928) Über den Farbensinn der Tagfalter. *Vergl. Phys.*, **8**, 658–692.

KNOLL, F. (1926) Die *Arum*-Blutenstände und ihre Besucher. *Abh. Zool-bot. Ges. Wien*, **12**, 381.

KUGLER, H. (1939) Sind Veronica und Circaea Schwebfliegenblumen? *Bot. Arch.*, **39**, 147–65.

KUGLER, H. (1943) Hummeln als Blütenbesucher. *Ergeb. Biol.*, **19**, 143–323.

KUGLER, H. (1956) Über die optische Wirkung von Fliegenblumen auf Fliegen. *Ber. d. bot. Gesell.*, **69**, 387–398.

LARSEN, P. and TUNG, S. M. (1950) Growth promoting and growth retarding substances in pollen from diploid and triploid apple varieties, *Bot. Gaz.*, **111**, 4, 436–447.

LEX, T. (1954) Duftmale an Blüten. *Z. vergl. Physiol.*, **36**, 212–234.

LIDFORS, B. (1896) Zur Biologie des Pollens. *Jahr. wiss. Bot.*, **29**, 1.

LINSLEY, E. G., MACSWAIN, J. W. and SMITH, R. F. (1955a) Observations on the nesting habits and flower relationships of some species of Melandrena. *Pan Pac. Ent.*, **31**, 173–185.

LINSLEY, E. G. and MACSWAIN, J. W. (1955b) The North American Andrenine bees of the subgenus Melandrena with descriptions of new species. *Pan Pac. Ent.*, **31**, 4, 163–172.

McCANN, C. (1931) On the fertilization of the flowers of the Sausage Tree (*Kigelia pinnata*, D.C.) by bats. *J. Bombay Nat. Hist. Soc.* **35**, 2, 467–471.

McCANN, C. (1942) Observations on Indian Duckweeds, Lemnaceae. *J. Bombay Nat. Hist. Soc.*, **43**, 2, 148–162.

McCANN, C. (1943) Light-windows in certain flowers (Asclepiadaceae and Araceae). *J. Bombay Nat. Hist. Soc.*, **44**, 2, 182–184.

McCANN, C. (1952) The Tui and its food plants. *Notornis*, July 6–14.

MADGE, M. A. (1929) Spermatogenesis and fertilization in the cleistogamous flower of *Viola odorata* var. *praecox* Hort. *Ann. Bot.*, **43**, 545–577.

MANNING, A. (1956) Some aspects of the foraging behaviour of bumblebees. *Behaviour*, **9**, 2–3, 164–201.

MANNING, A. (1957) Some evolutionary aspects of the flower constancy of bees. *Proc. R. Phys. Soc.*, **25**, 3, 67–71.

MAURIZIO, A. (1951) Untersuchungen über den Einfluss der Pollenernährung und Brutflege auf die Lebensdauer und den physiologischen Zustand der Bienen. Report of the XIVth Int. Beekeeping Congr. p. 320, Leamington.

MAURIZIO, A. (1954) Untersuchungen über die Nektarsekretion einiger polyploider Kulturpflanzen. *Arch. J. Klaus-Stiftung*, **29**, 340.

MAURIZIO, A. (1958) Pollenkeimung hemmende Stoffe im Körper der Honigbiene. XVII Int. Beekeeping Congr.

MELIN, D. (1935) Contributions to the study of the theory of selection II. The problem of Ornithophily. *Uppsala Univ. Ark.*, **16**, 1–338.

MENKE, H. F. (1951) Insect pollination of apples in Washington State. Report of the XIVth Int. Beekeeping Congr., Leamington.

MOEWUS, F. (1950) The physiology and biochemistry of the self-sterility in Forsythia. *Report Int. Bot. Congr. Stockholm*, p. 777.

NUR, N. (1958) Observations with *Musa textilis* Née. *Cont. Gen. Agric. Res. Stn.*, *Bogor*, **151**, 1–115.

PALMER, T. P. (1962) Population structure, breeding system, interspecific hybridization and allopolyploidy. *Heredity*, **17**, 2, 278–283.

PEDERSEN, M. W. (1961) Lucerne pollination. *Bee World*, **42**, 6, 145–149.

PERCIVAL, M. S. (1962) Types of nectar in Angiosperms. *New Phyt.*, **60**, 235–281.

PIJL, L. VAN DER (1941) Flagelliflory and cauliflory and adaptations to bats in Mucuna and other plants. *Ann. Bot. Gdn. Buitenzorg*, **51**, 83–98.

PIJL, L. VAN DER (1954) Xylocopa and flowers in the tropics I, II and III. *Proc. Kon. Ned. Ak. v. Wet.*, ser. C. **57**, 4, 413–423; 5, 541–562.

POHL, F. (1937) Die Pollenerzeugung der Windblütler. *Beih. bot. Centrbl. Abt. A.* **56**,

PORSCH, O. (1926) Kritische Quellenstudien über Blumenbesuch durch Vögel i. *Biol. Gen.*, **2**, 3, 217–240.

PORSCH, O. (1954) Geschlechtgebundener Blütenduft. *Oest. bot. Z.*, **101**, 4, 359–372.

PORSCH, O. (1956) Windpollen und Blumeninsekt. *Oest. bot. Z.*, **103**, 1, 1–18.

RAW, G. R. (1953) The effect on nectar secretion of removing nectar from flowers. *Bee World*, **34**, 2, 23–25.

RESENDE, F. (1950) Contribution to the physiology of development of the inflorescence and of the single flower. *Portug. Acta Biol.* (R.B. Goldschmidt Vol) 729–84.

ROBERTSON, C. (1922) Synopsis of the Panurgidae (Hymenoptera). *Psyche*, **29**, 159–173.

ROBERTSON, C. (1923) Flower visits of insects I. *Psyche*, **30**, 158–169.

ROBERTSON, C. (1924) Flower visits of insects. II. *Psyche*, **31**, 93–111.

ROBERTSON, C. (1925) Habits of the Hibiscus Bee, *Emphor bombiformis*. *Psyche*, **32**, 278–282.

RYLE, M. (1954) The influence of nitrogen, phosphate and potash on the secretion of nectar. II. *J. Agric. Sci.*, **44**, 408–419.

SARGENT, O. H. (1928) Reactions between birds and plants. *Emu*, **27**, 185–192.

SCHREMMER, F. (1953) Observations on the biology of Labiate flowers (nectar and pollen stealing). *Oest. bot. Z.*, **100** (1/2) 18–24.

SCHREMMER, F. (1960) *Acanthus mollis*, eine europäische Holzbienen-blume. *Oest. bot. Z.*, **107**, 1, 84–105.

SCHREMMER. F. (1963) Blütenbiologische beobachtungen an Labiaten. *Oest. bot. Z.*, **100**, 8–24.

SCOTT-ELLIOT, G. F. (1889–90) Ornithophilous flowers in South Africa. *Ann. Bot.*, **4**, 265–280.

SHUEL, R. W. (1955) Nectar secretion in relation to nitrogen supply, nutritional status, and growth of the plant. *Can. J. Agr. Sci.*, **34**, 2.

SHUEL, R. W. (1956) Studies of nectar secretion in excised flowers I. The influence of cultural conditions on quantity and composition of nectar. *Can. J. Bot.*, **34**, 142–153.

SHUEL, R. W. (1957) Some aspects of the relation between nectar secretion and nitrogen, phosphorous and potassium nutrition. *Can. J. Plant Sci.*, **37**, 220–236.

SRIVASTAVA, D. N. (1937) Studies in the nonsetting of pears. III. The effect of flower characters. *East Malling Res. Sta. Rep.*, **25**, 145–153.

STADLER, S. (1886) Beiträge zur Kenntnis der Nektarien und Biologie der Blüten. Zürich, Dissertation.

TODD, F. E. and BRETHERICK, O. (1942) The composition of pollens. *J. Econ. Ent.*, **35**, 312–317.

UPHOF, J. C. TH. (1938) Cleistogamic flowers. *Bot. Rev.*, **4**, 21–49.

VANSELL, G. H., WATKINS, W. G. and BISHOP, R. K. (1942) Orange nectar and pollen in relation to bee activity. *J. Econ. Ent.*, **35**, 3, 321–23.

VOGEL, S. (1954) Blutenbiologische Typen als Elemente der Sippen-gliederung. *Bot. Studien*, **1**, Jena.

WADEY, H. J. (1961) Nectar yield and age. *Bee Craft*, **43**, 8, 86.

WAKEFIELD, N. (1960) Nectar flowers and honeyeaters. *Victorian Nat.*, **77**, 1, 22.

WALKER, L. W. and YOUNG, A. S. (1934) Humming Bird Haven. *Nat. Hist.*, **34**, 133–140.

WILLIS, J. C. (1901) Studies in the morphology and ecology of the Podostemaceae of Ceylon and India. *Ann. R. Bot. Gdns. Peradenyia*, **1**, 4, 267–465.

WILLIS, J. C. and BURKHILL, I. H. (1895) Flowers and Insects in Great Britain. *Ann. Bot.*, **9**, 227–273.

WOOD, W. M. L. (1953) Thermonasty in tulip and crocus flowers. *J. Exp. Bot.*, **4**, 10, 65–77.

WYKES, G. R. (1952a) The preferences of honeybees for solutions of various sugars which occur in nectar. *J. Exp. Biol.*, **29**, 4, 511–18.

WYKES, G. R. (1952b) An investigation of the sugars present in the nectar of flowers of various species. *New Phytol.*, **51**, 2, 210–15.

ZIMMERMANN, M. (1953) Papierchromatographische Untersuchungen über die pflanzliche Zuckersekretion. *Ber. Schweiz. Bot. Ges.*, **63**, 402–429.

ZIMMERMANN, M. (1954) Über die Sekretion saccharoespaltender Transglukosidasen im pflanzlichen Necktar. *Experientia*, **10**, 3, 145–146.

BIBLIOGRAPHY

ARBER, A. (1920) *Water Plants*. Cambridge Univ. Press.

BEEBE, W. (1950) *High Jungle*. Bodley Head, London.

CAMMERLOHER, H. (1931) *Blutenbiologie I. Bornträger*, Berlin.

CARTHY, T. D. (1956) *Animal Navigation*. Allen & Unwin, London.

CAYLEY, N. W. (1958) *What Bird is That? Guide to the Birds of Australia*. 2nd ed. All-Pets.

CLAPHAM, A. R., TUTIN, T. G. and WARBURG, E. F. (1962) *Flora of the British Isles*. Cambridge Univ. Press.

DARLINGTON, C. D. and WYLIE, A. P. (1955) *Chromosome Atlas of Flowering Plants*. 2nd edition, Allen & Unwin, London.

DARWIN, C. (1862) *The Various Contrivances by which Orchids are fertilized by Insects*. Murray, London.

DARWIN, C. (1880) *The Different Forms of Flowers on Plants of the same Species*. Murray, London.

ELTRINCHAM, H. (1933) *The Senses of Insects*. Methuen, London.

FORD, E. B. (1945) *Butterflies*. Collins, London.

FORD, E. B. (1955) *Moths*. Collins, London.

FREE, J. B. and BUTLER, C. G. (1959) *Bumblebees*. Collins, London.

FRISCH, K. VON (1950) *Bees*. Cornell Univ. Press, New York.

FRISCH, K. VON (1960) *"Sprache" und Orientierung der Bienen*. A. Wander Gedenkvorlesung 3.

GILLIARD, E. T. (1958) *Living Birds of the World*. Doubleday.

GREENEWALT, C. H. (1960) *Hummingbirds*. Doubleday, New York.

HAMPTON, F. A. (1925) *The Scent of Flowers and Leaves*. Dulau, London.

HERROD-HEMPSALL W. (1943) The Anatomy, Physiology and Natural History of the Honeybee. *Brit. Bee J.*, London.

219

HODGES, D. (1952) *The Pollen Loads of the Honeybee.* Bee Res. Ass., London.

IMMS, A. D. (1947) *Insect Natural History.* Collins, London.

IMMS, A. D. (1946) *Textbook of Entomology.* Methuen, London.

JAEGER, P. (1961) *The Wonderful Life of Flowers.* Harrap, London.

JAMES, W. O. and CLAPHAM, A. R. (1935) *The Biology of Flowers.* Clarendon Press, Oxford.

KERNER, V. M. (1894–95) *The Natural History of Plants.* 2 vols. Trans. F. W. Oliver. Blackie, London.

KNUTH, P. (1906–9) *Handbook of Flower Pollination.* 3 vols. Trans. J. R. Ainsworth Davis. Clarendon Press, Oxford.

KUGLER, H. (1955) *Einführung in die Blütenekologie.* Gustav Fischer, Stuttgart.

LOVELL, J. H. (1920) *The Flower and the Bee.* Constable, London.

MACKWORTH-PRAED, C. W. (1955) Birds of Eastern and North Eastern Africa. *African Handbook of Birds.* Ser. 1, vol. 2.

MÜLLER, H. (1883) *The Fertilization of Flowers.* Macmillan, London.

ROSSER, E. M. (1952) A study of nectar secretion in Fuchsia. Ph.D. Thesis, University of London.

SERVENTY, D. L. and WHITTELL, H. M. (1951) *Handbook of the Birds of Western Australia.* Patersons.

SKENE, M. (1932) *The Biology of Flowering Plants.* Sidgwick & Jackson, London.

SLADEN, F. W. L. (1912) *The Humblebee.* Macmillan, London.

SNODGRASS, R. E. (1925) *Anatomy and Physiology of the Honeybee.* McGraw-Hill, New York.

SOUTH, R. (n.d.) *The Butterflies and Moths of the British Isles.* Warne, London.

STEBBINS, G. L. (1950) *Variation and Evolution in Plants.* London: Geoffrey Cumberlege. Oxford University Press.

SUMMERHAYES, V. S. (1951) *Wild Orchids of Britain.* Collins, London.

WIGGLESWORTH, V. B. (1939) *The Principles of Insect Physiology.* Methuen, London.

ANIMAL INDEX

PLANT INDEX

227

SUBJECT INDEX